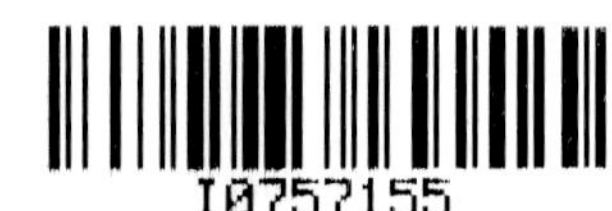

This Book Belongs To:

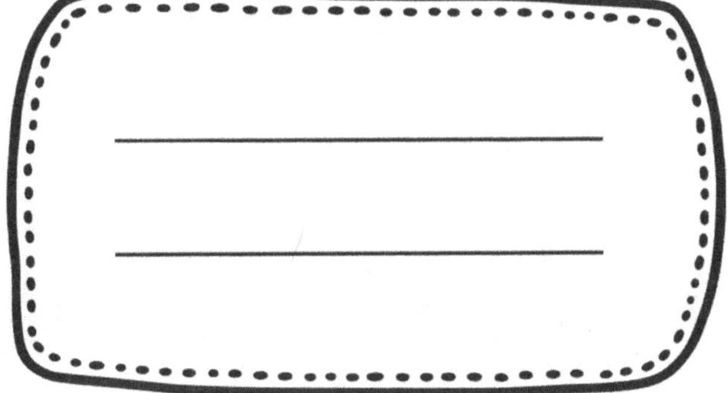

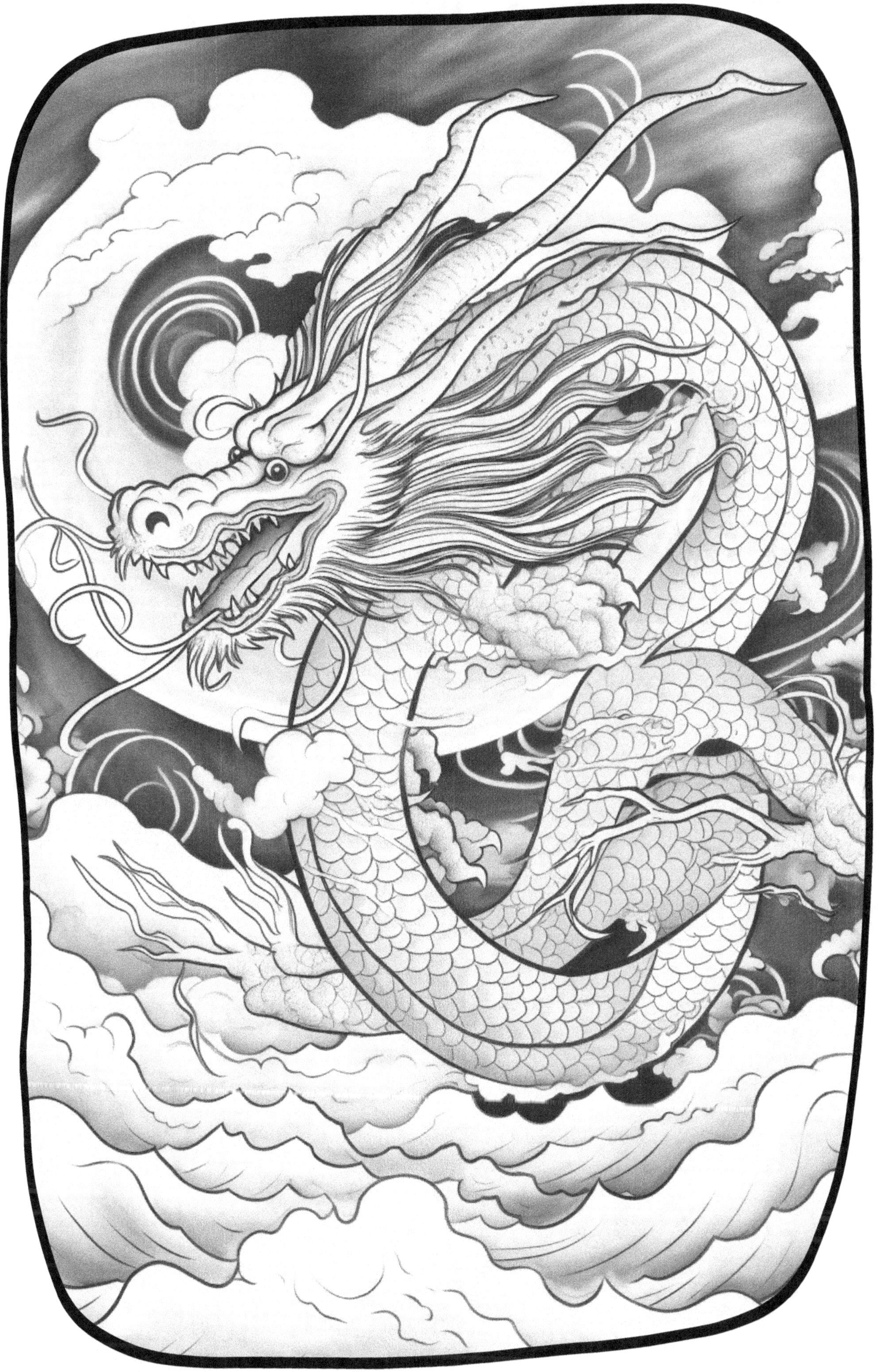

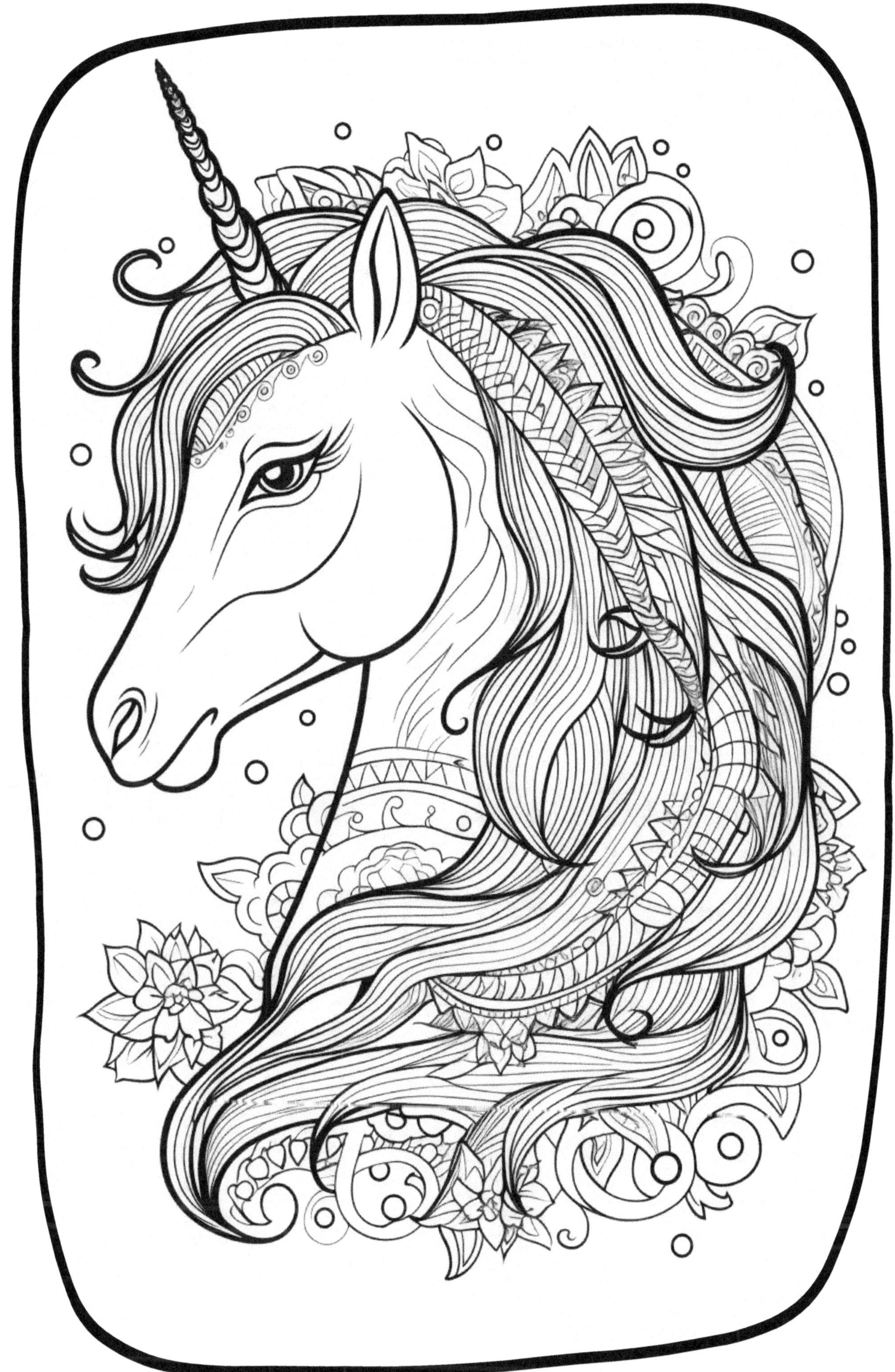

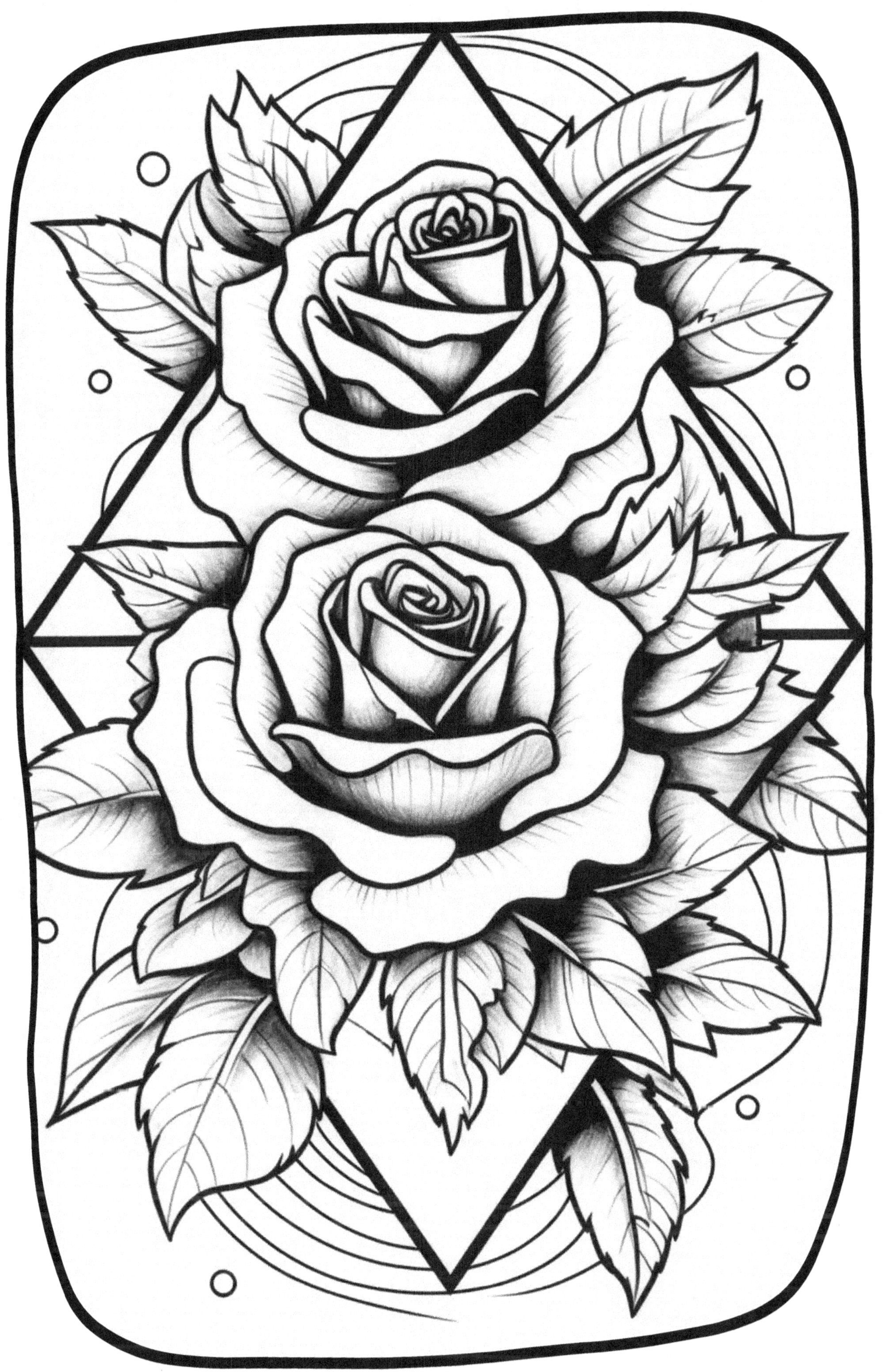

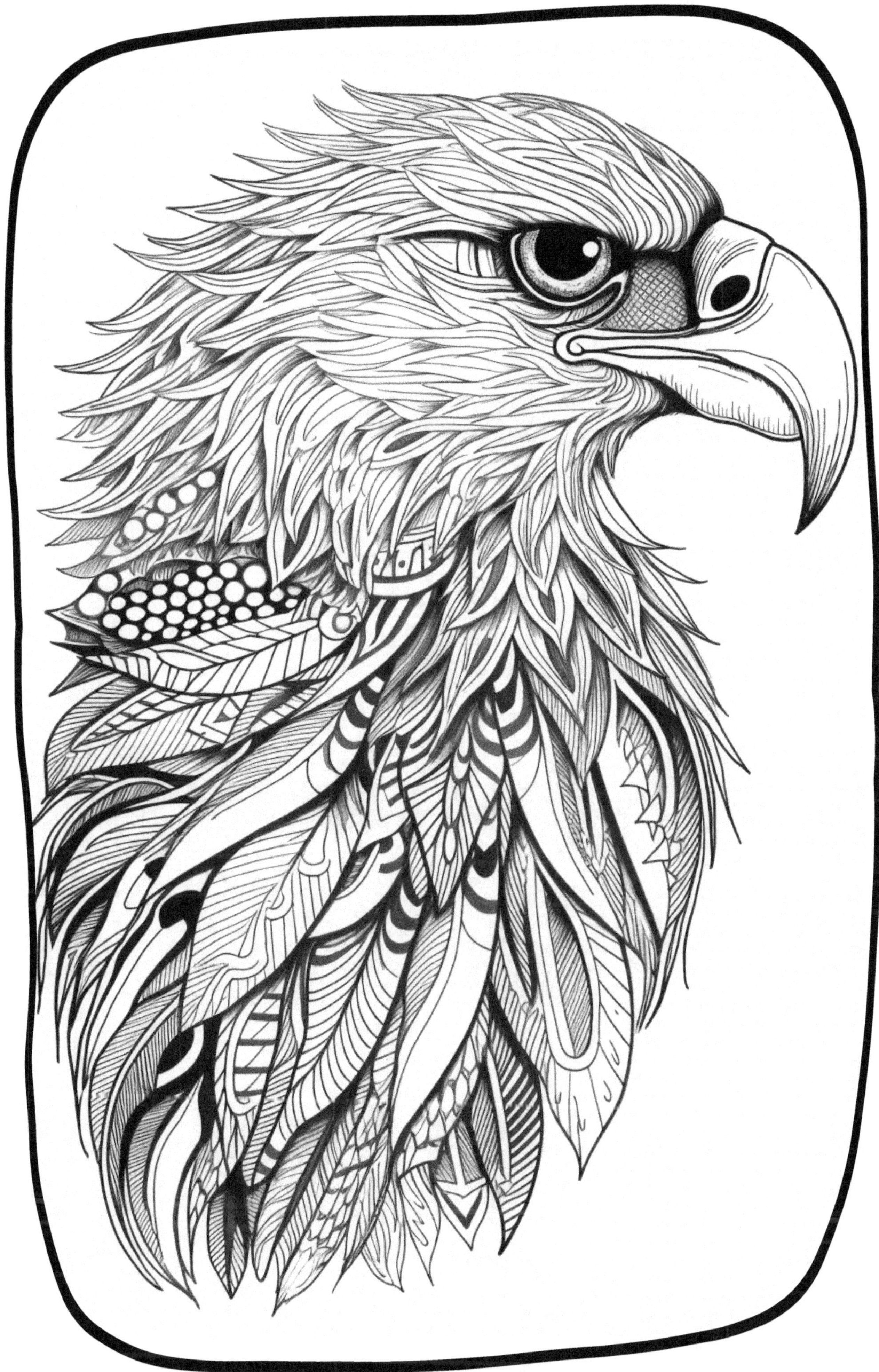

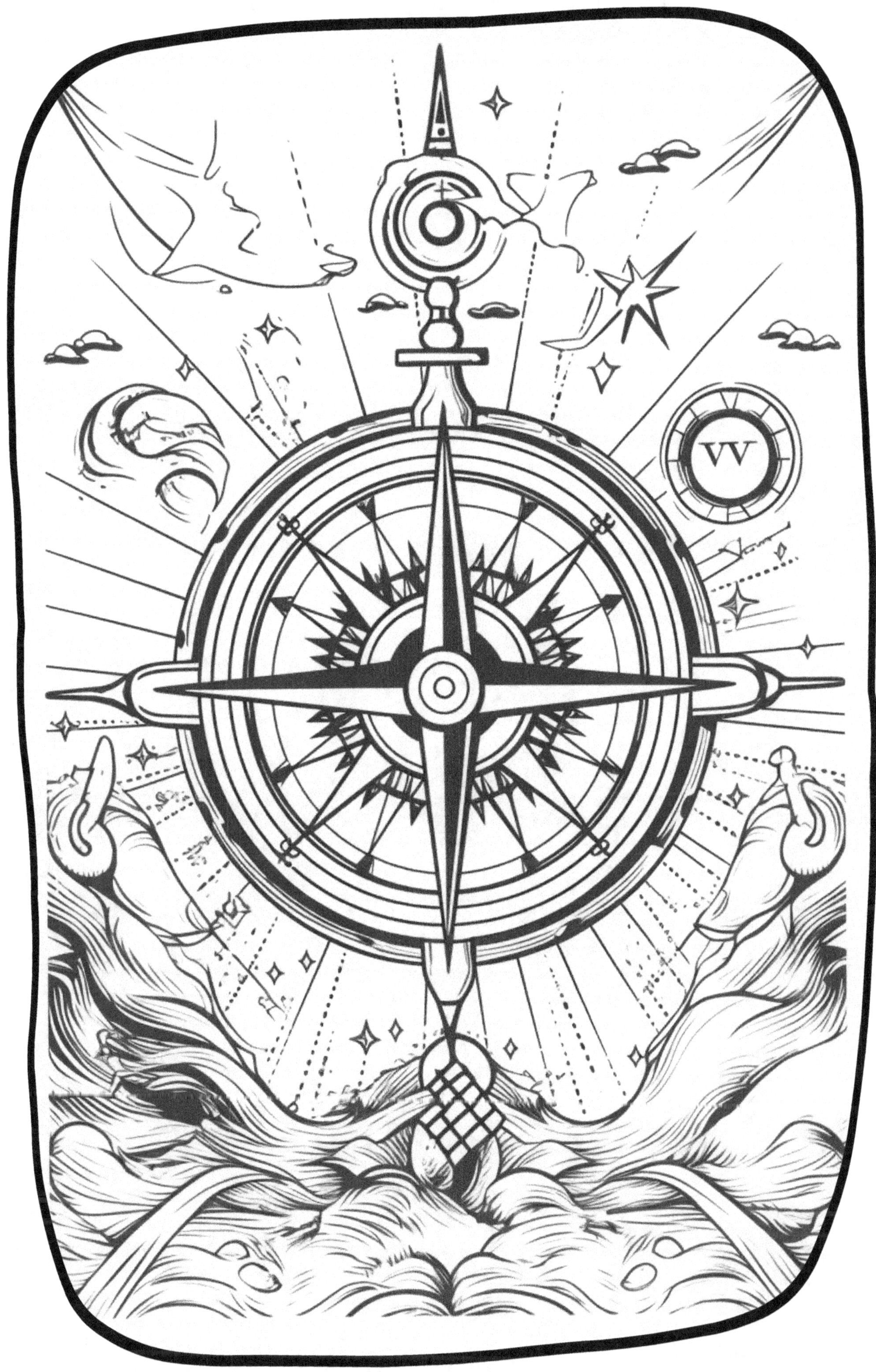
W

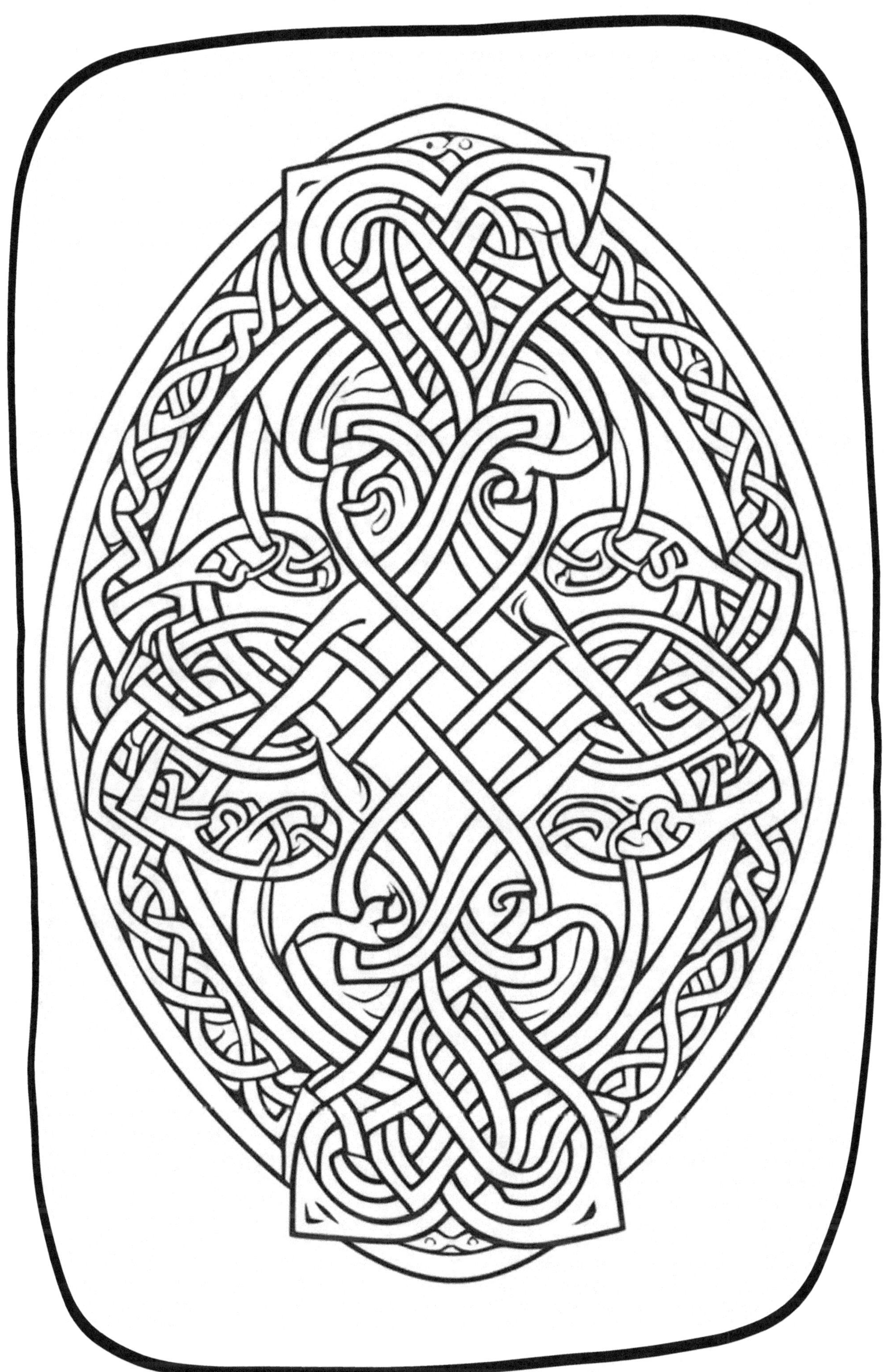

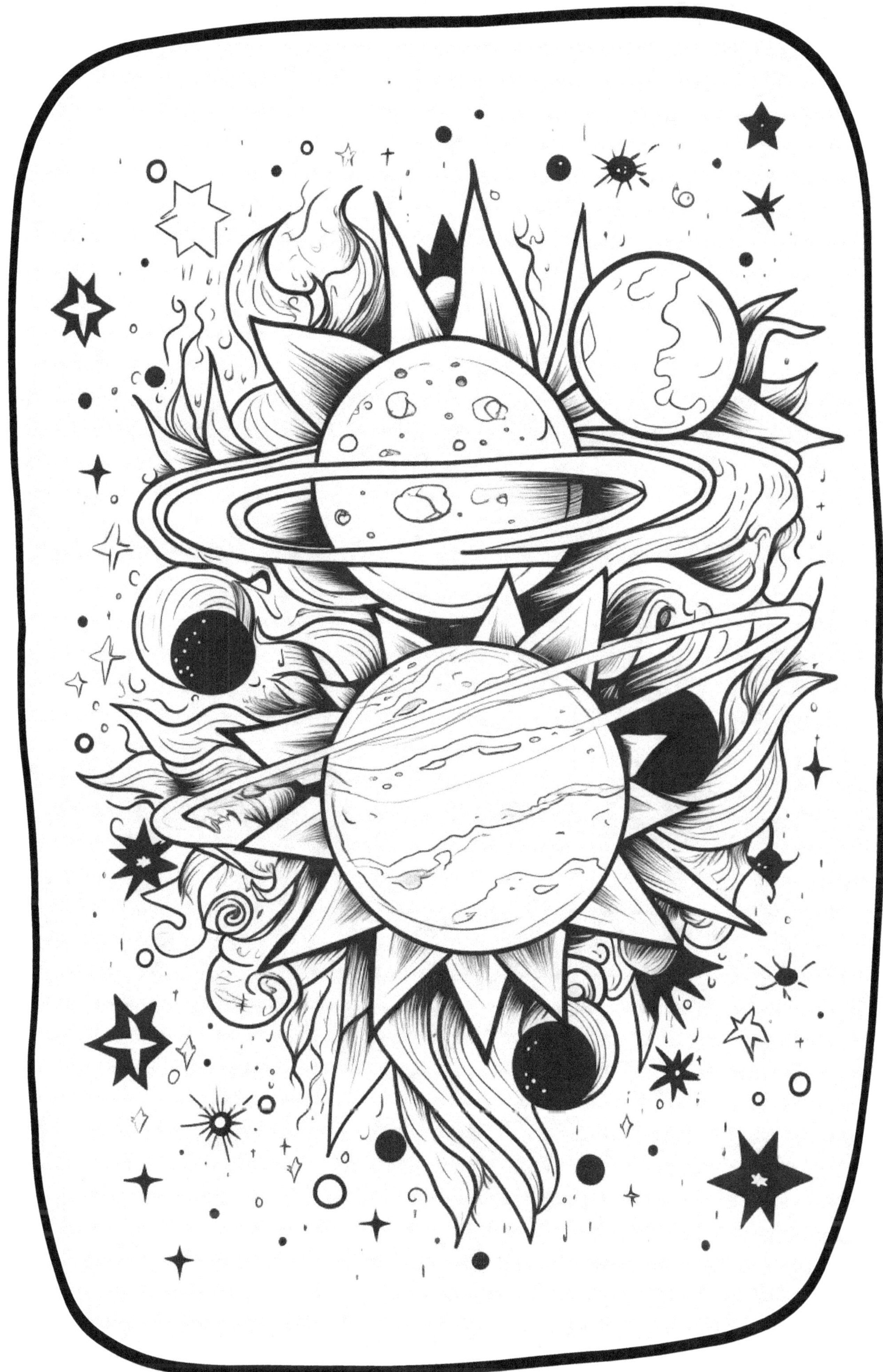

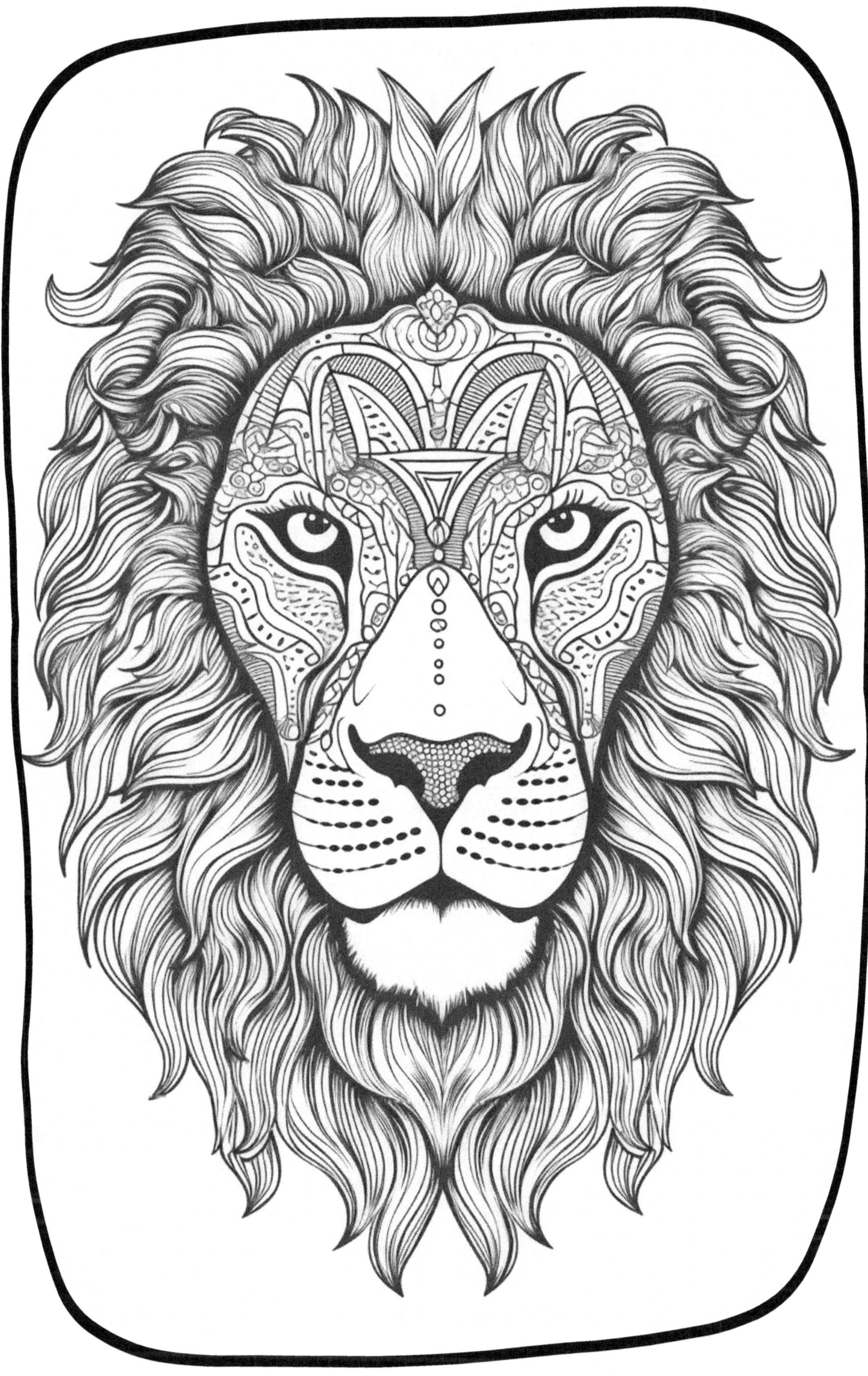

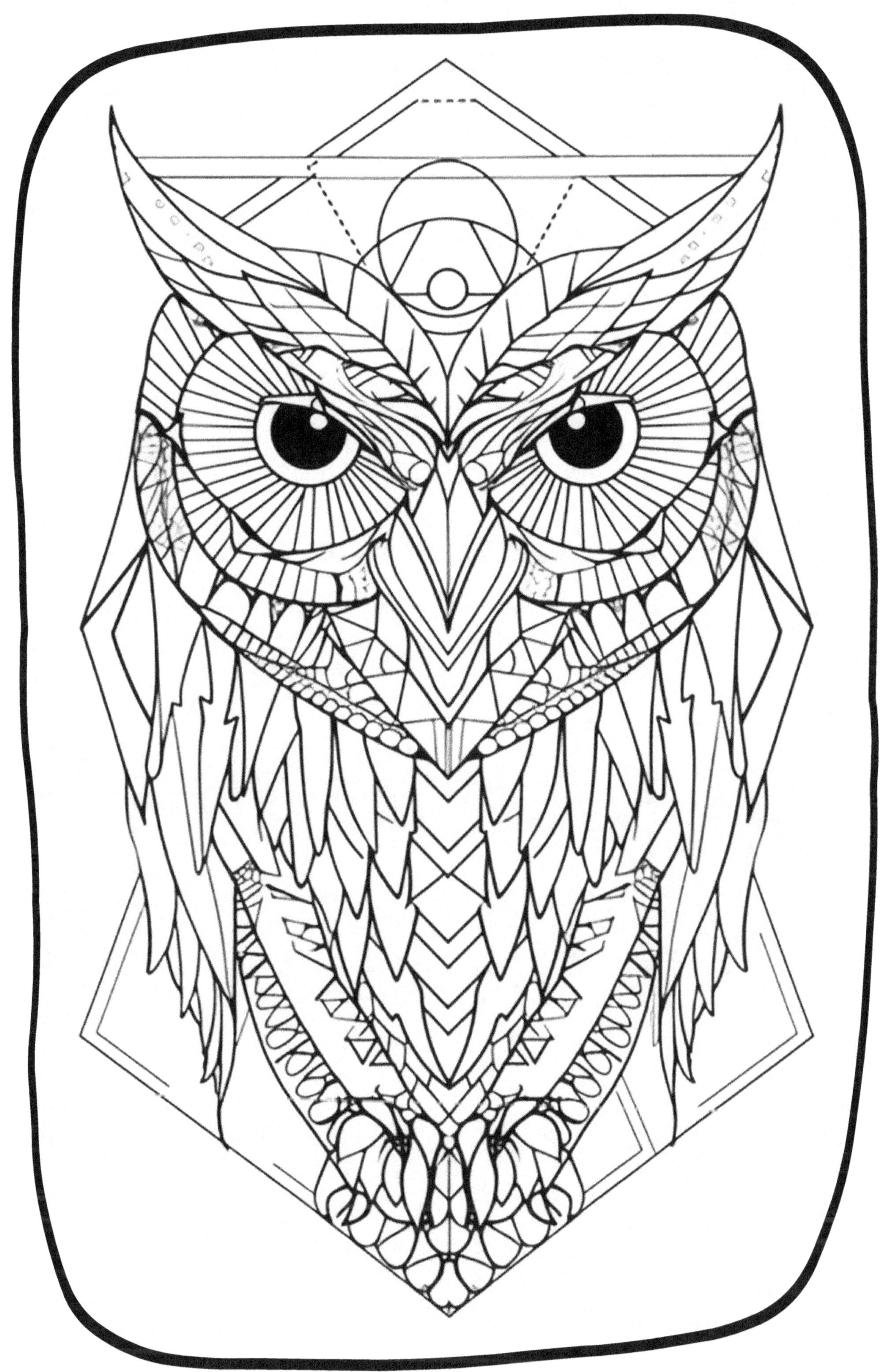

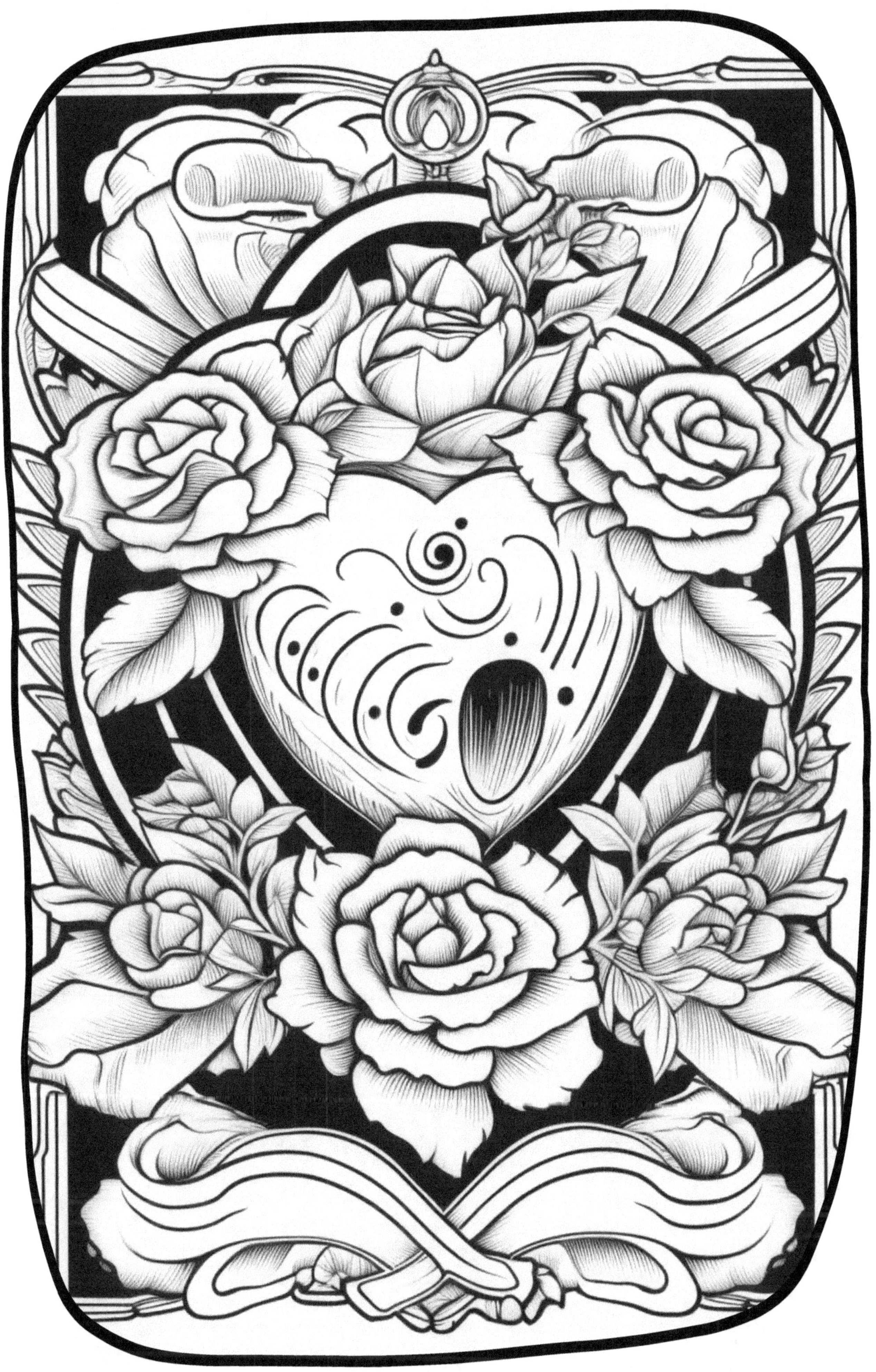

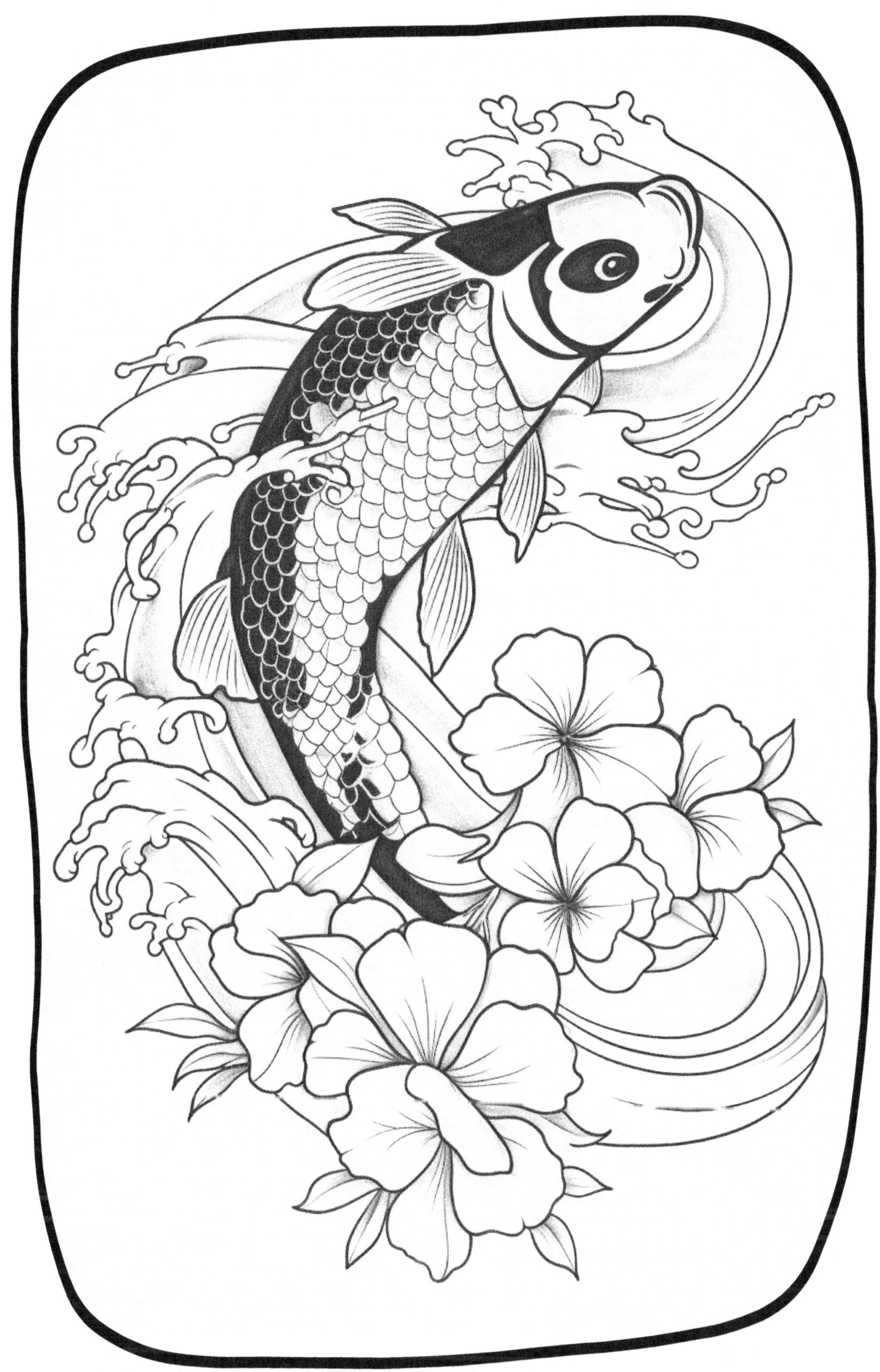

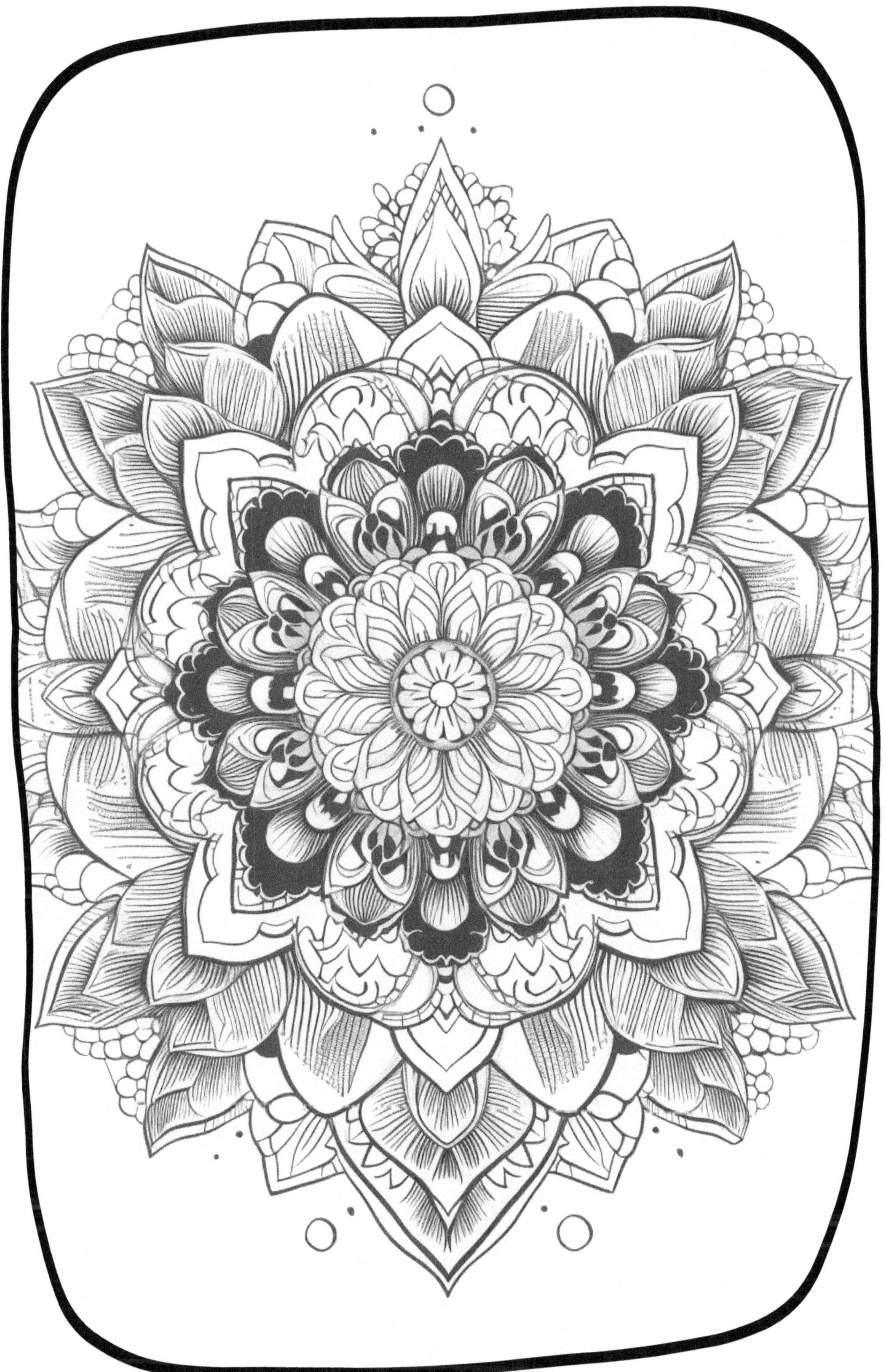

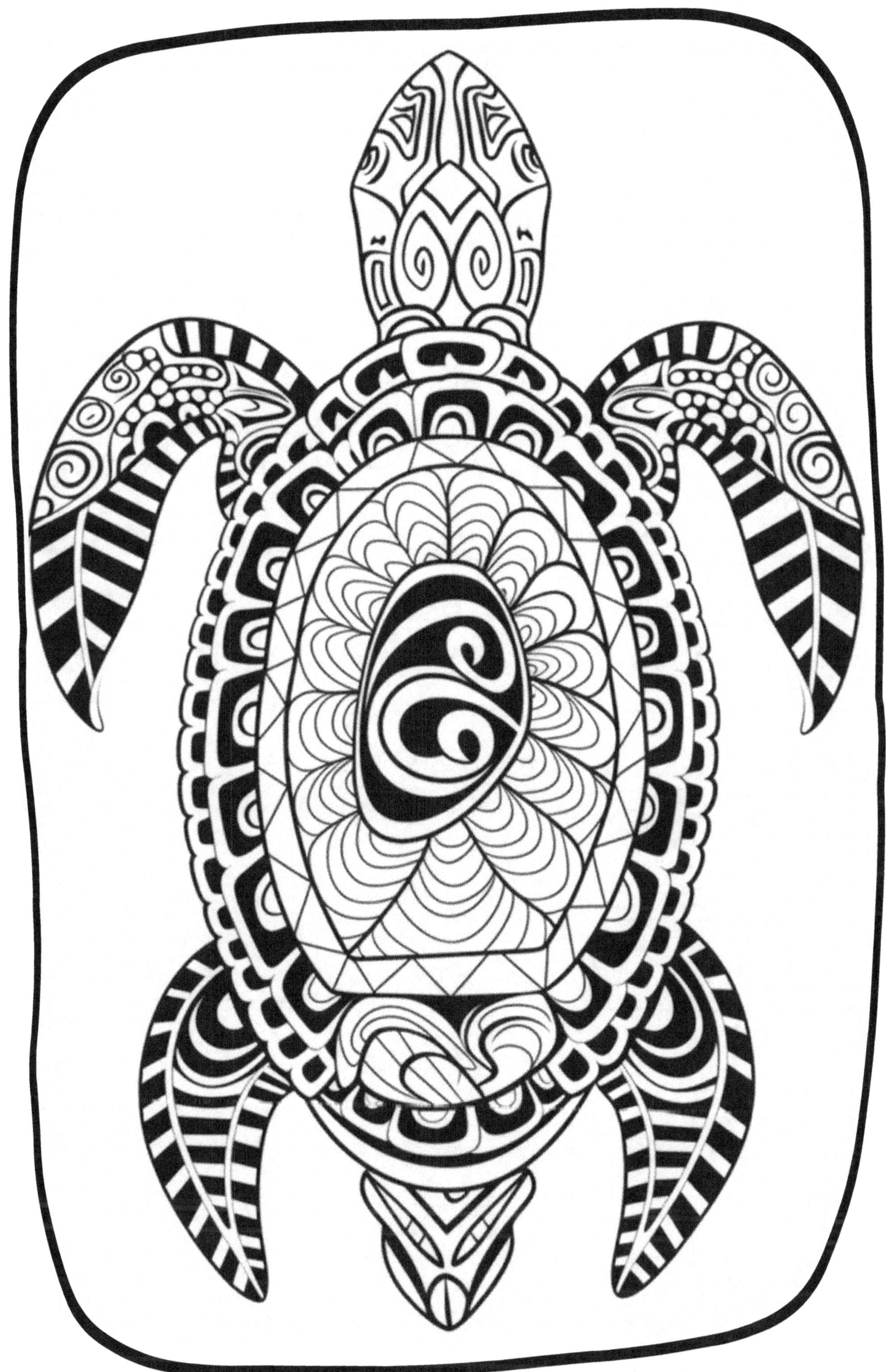

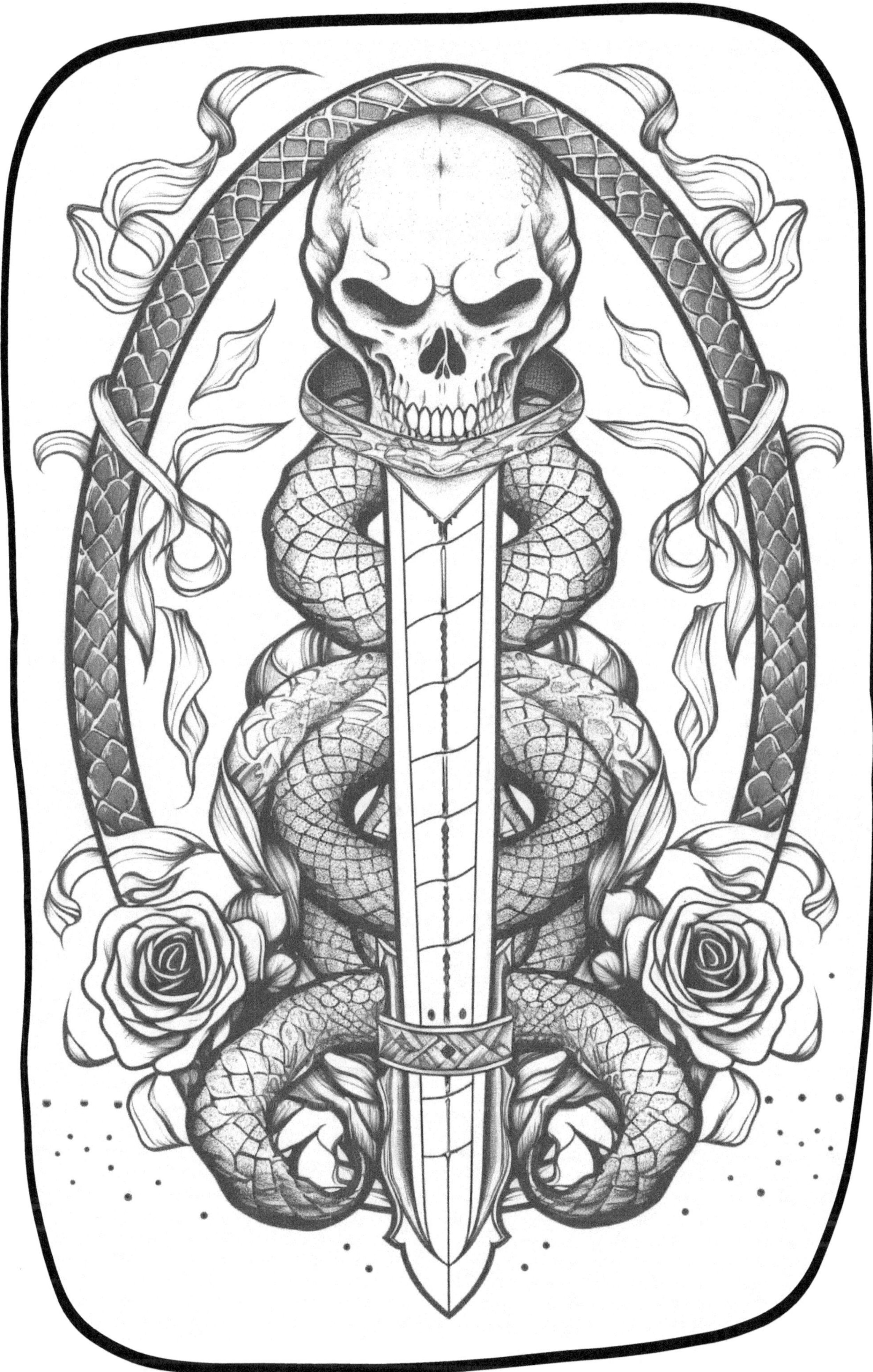

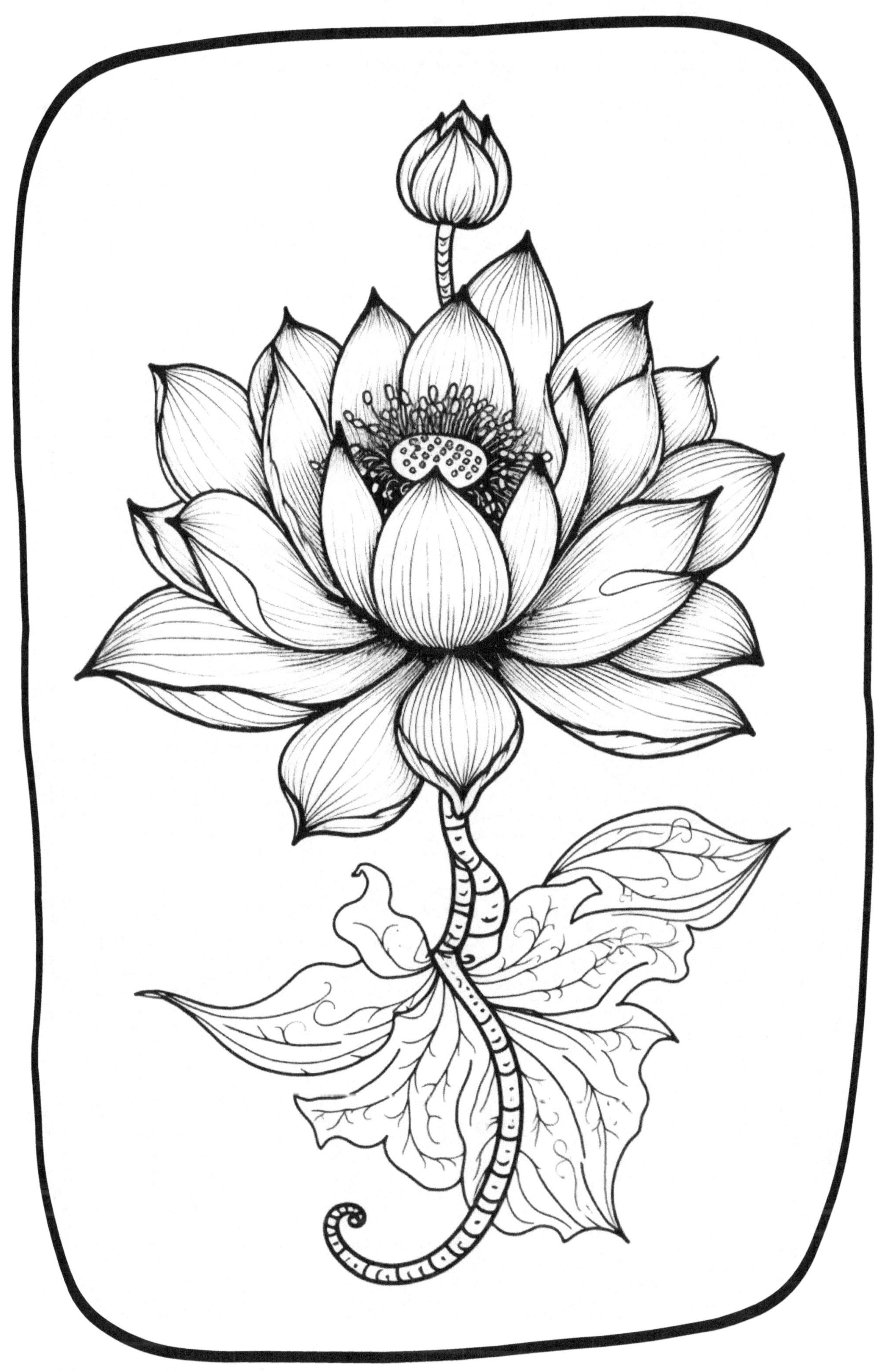

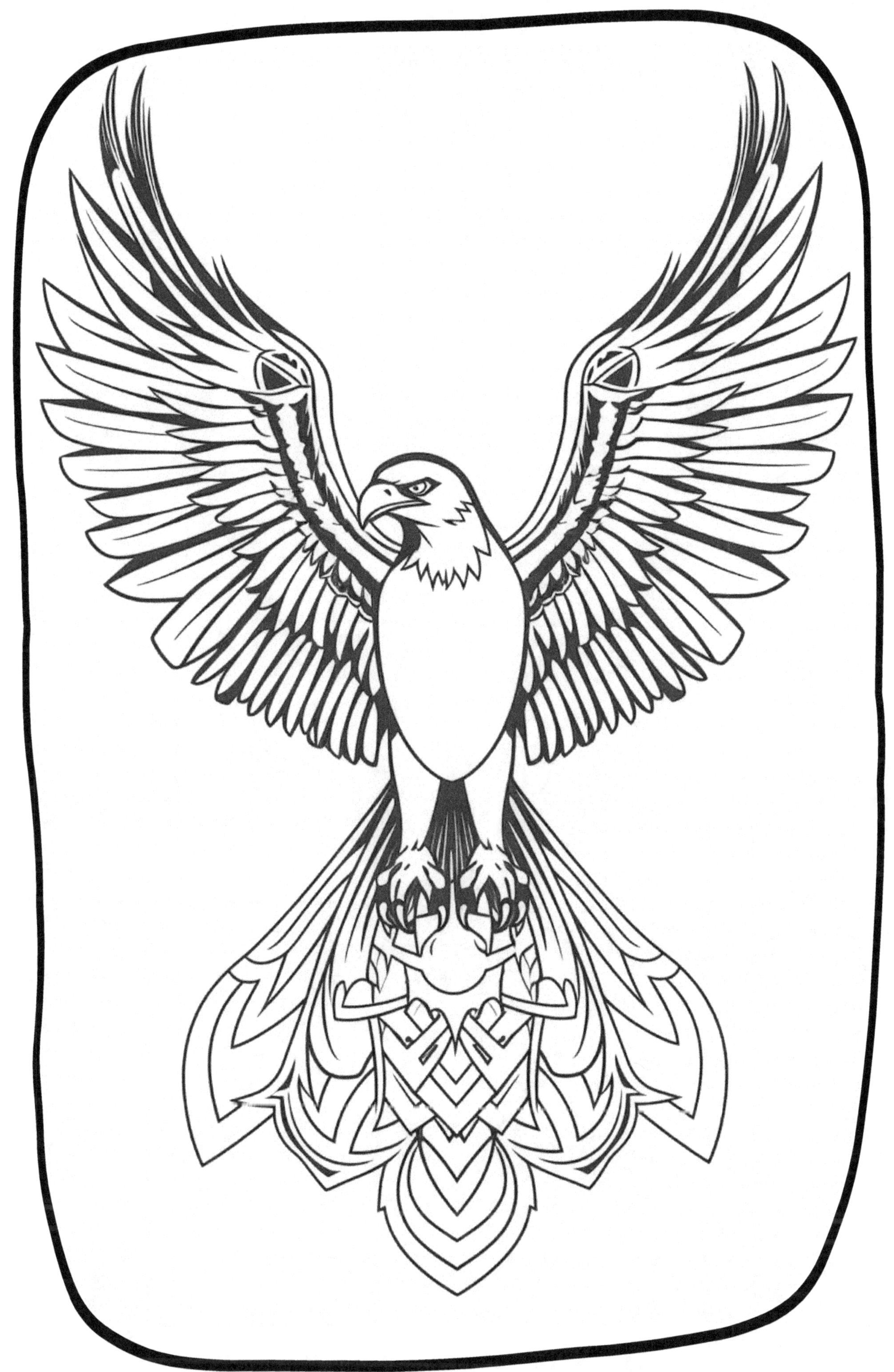

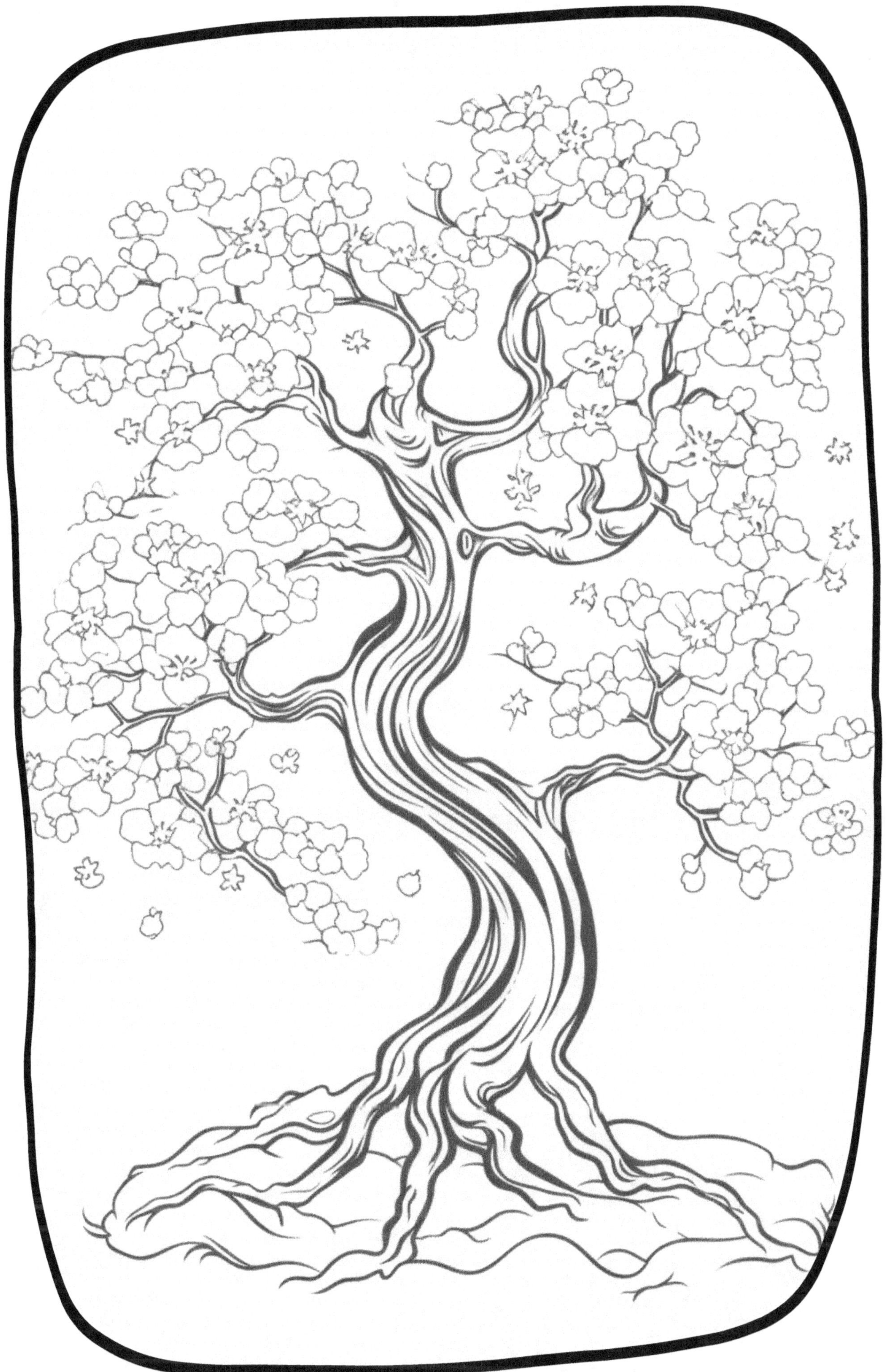

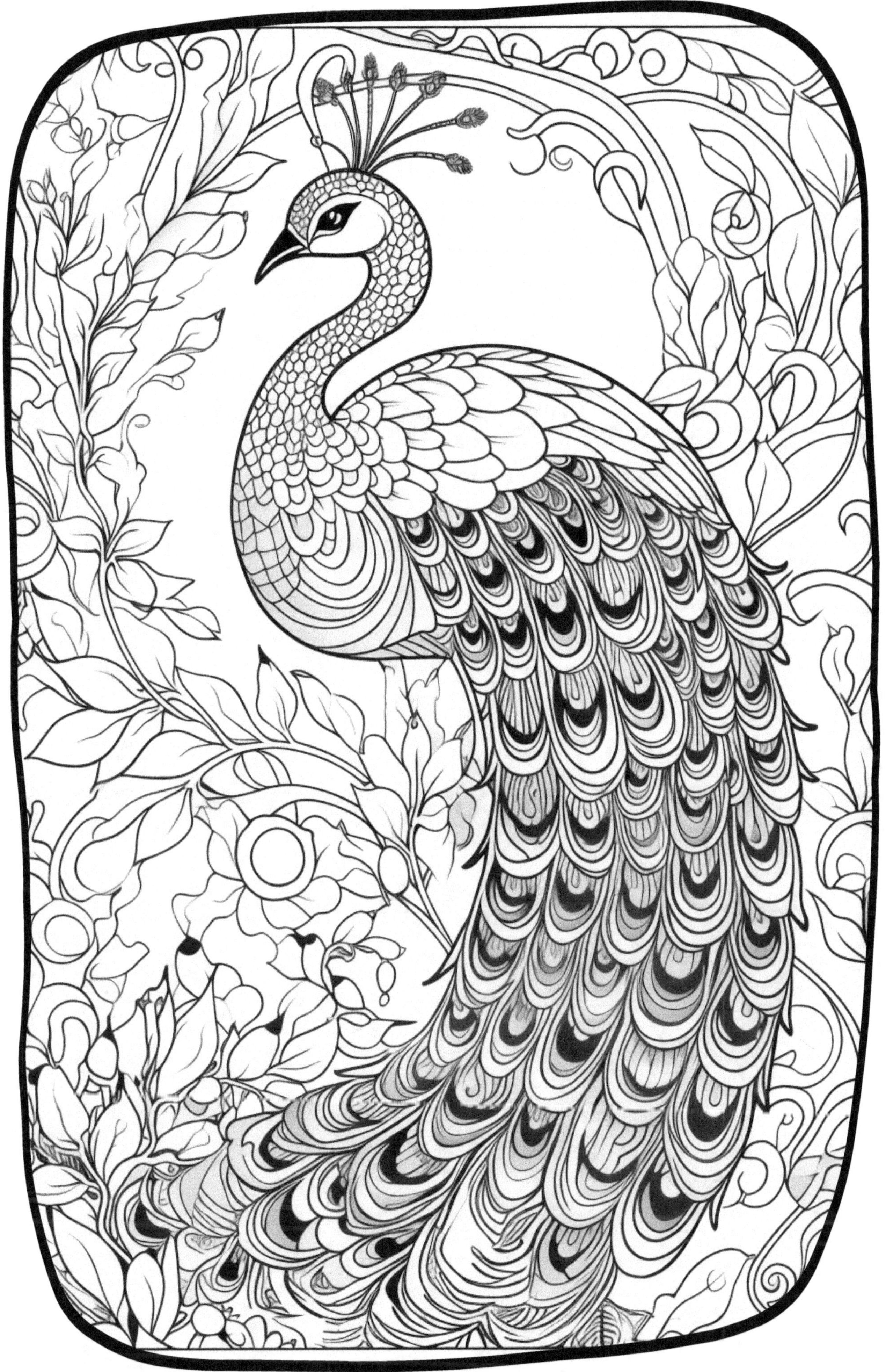

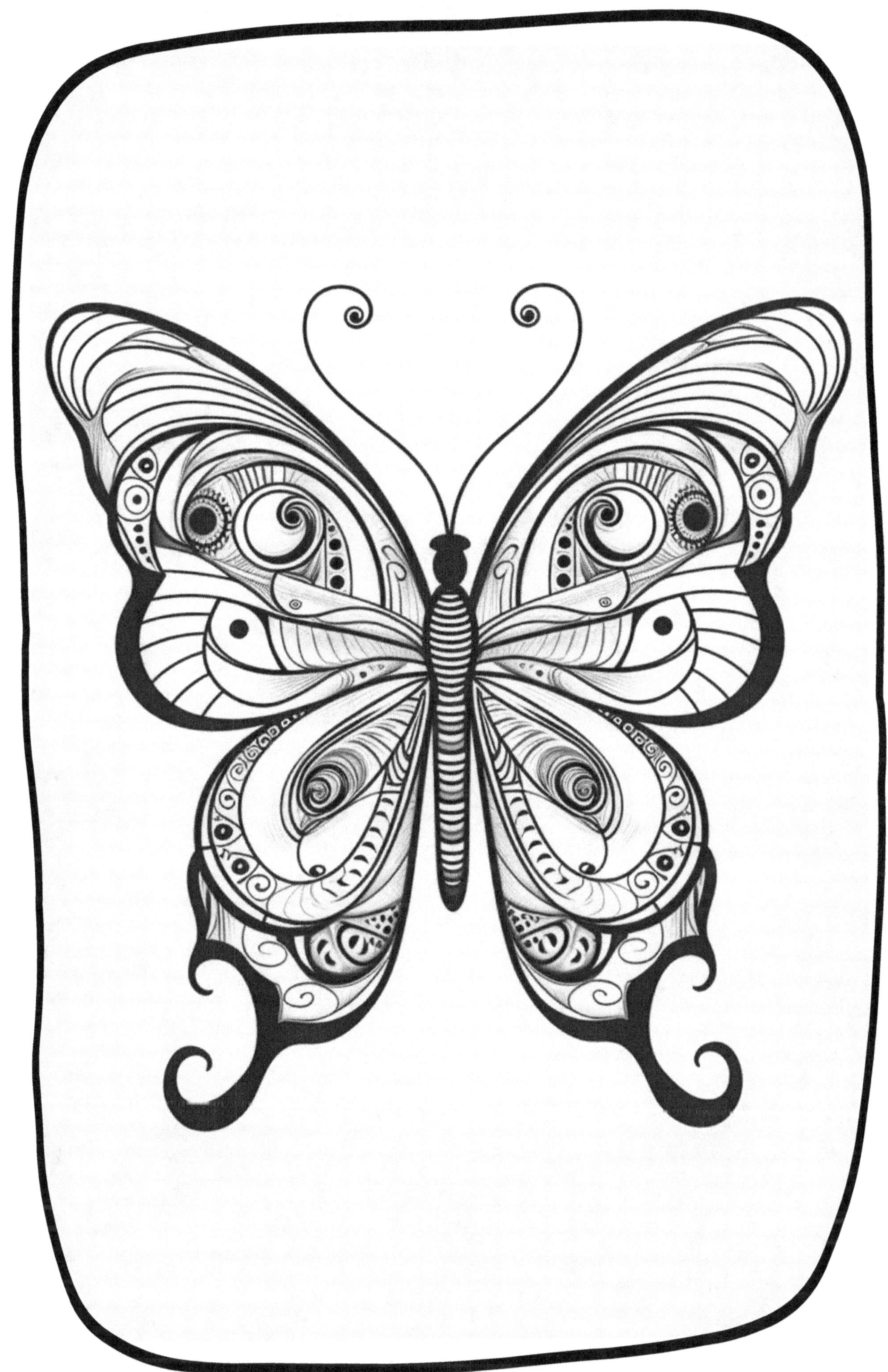

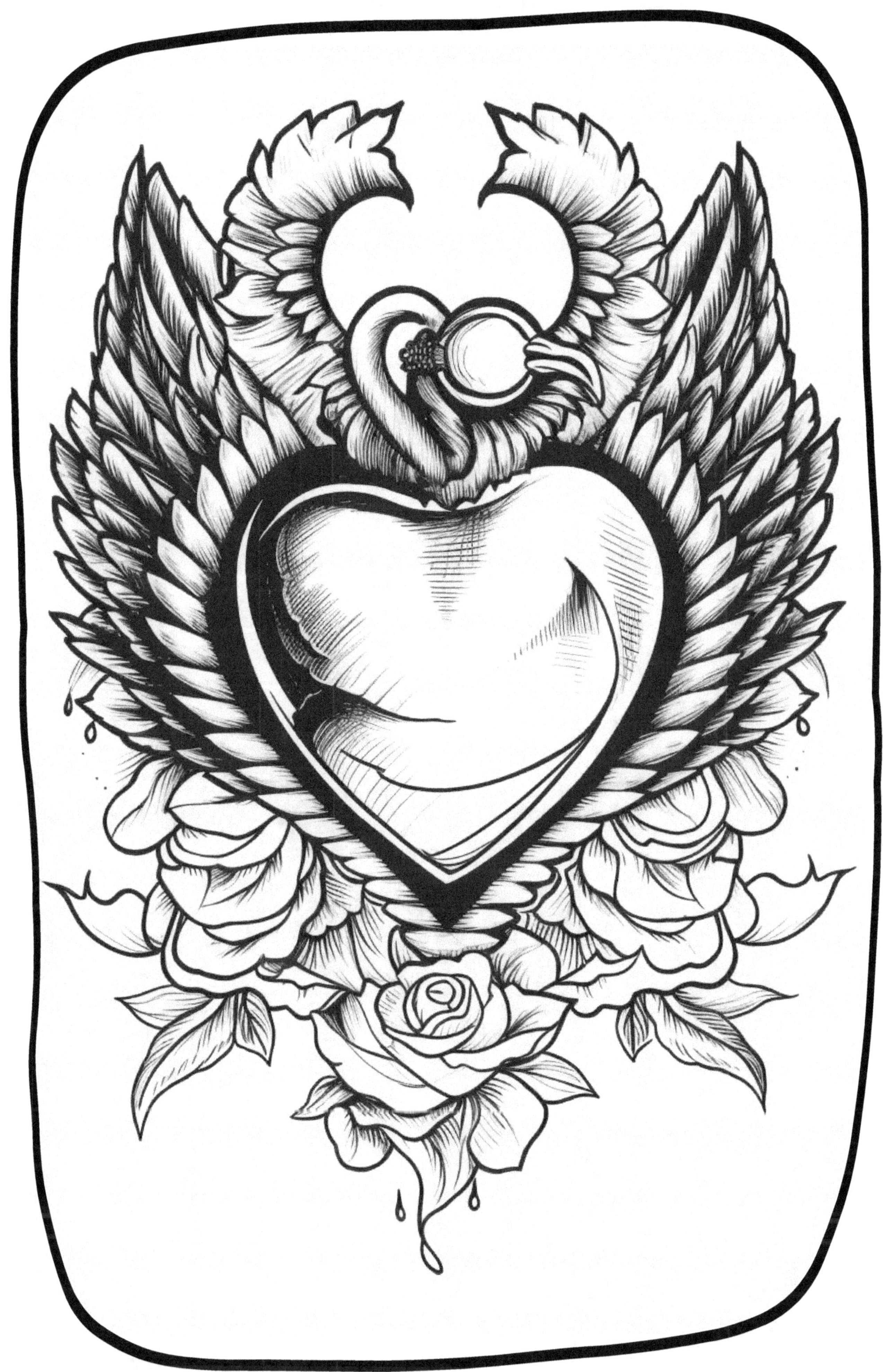

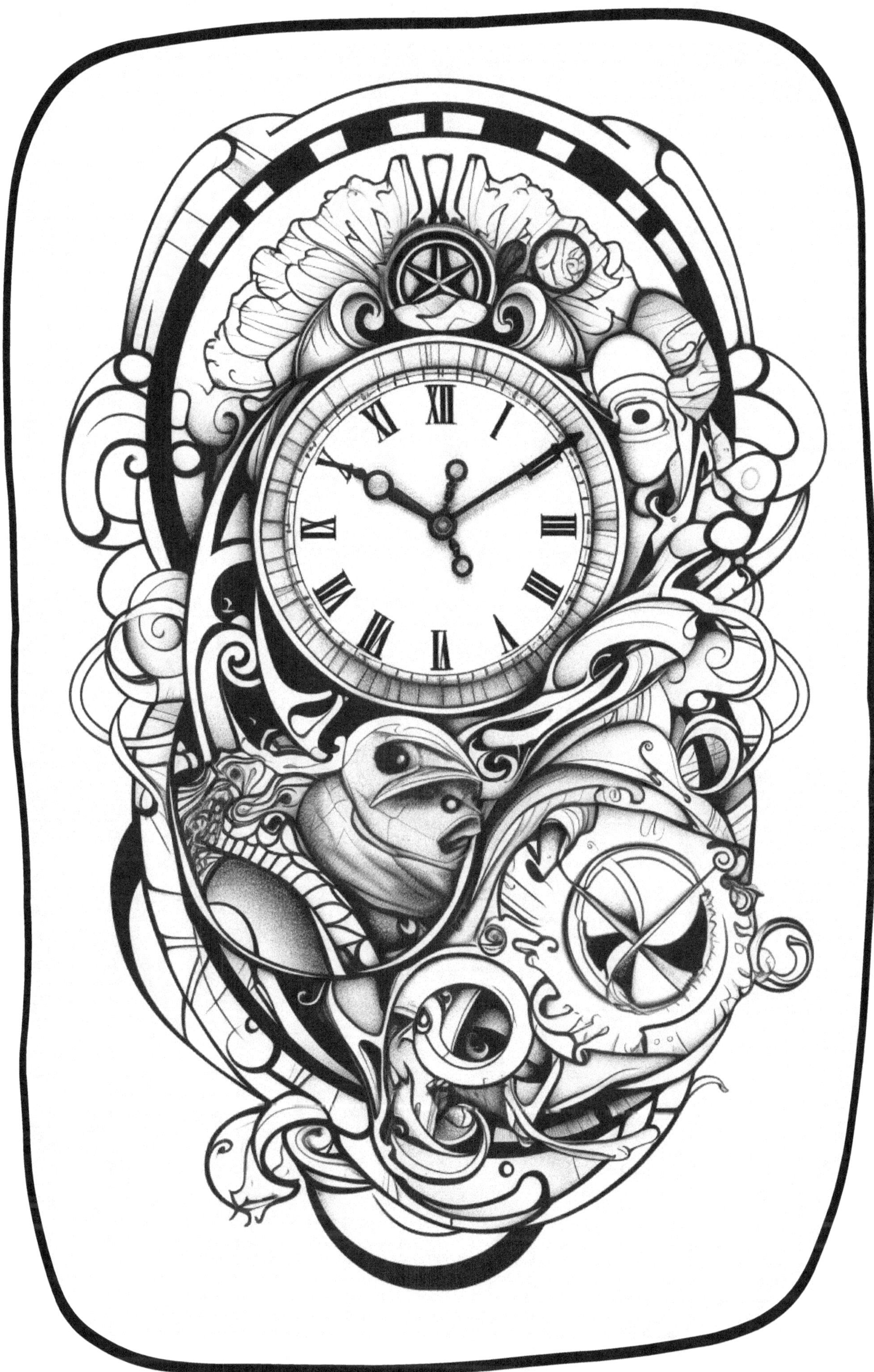

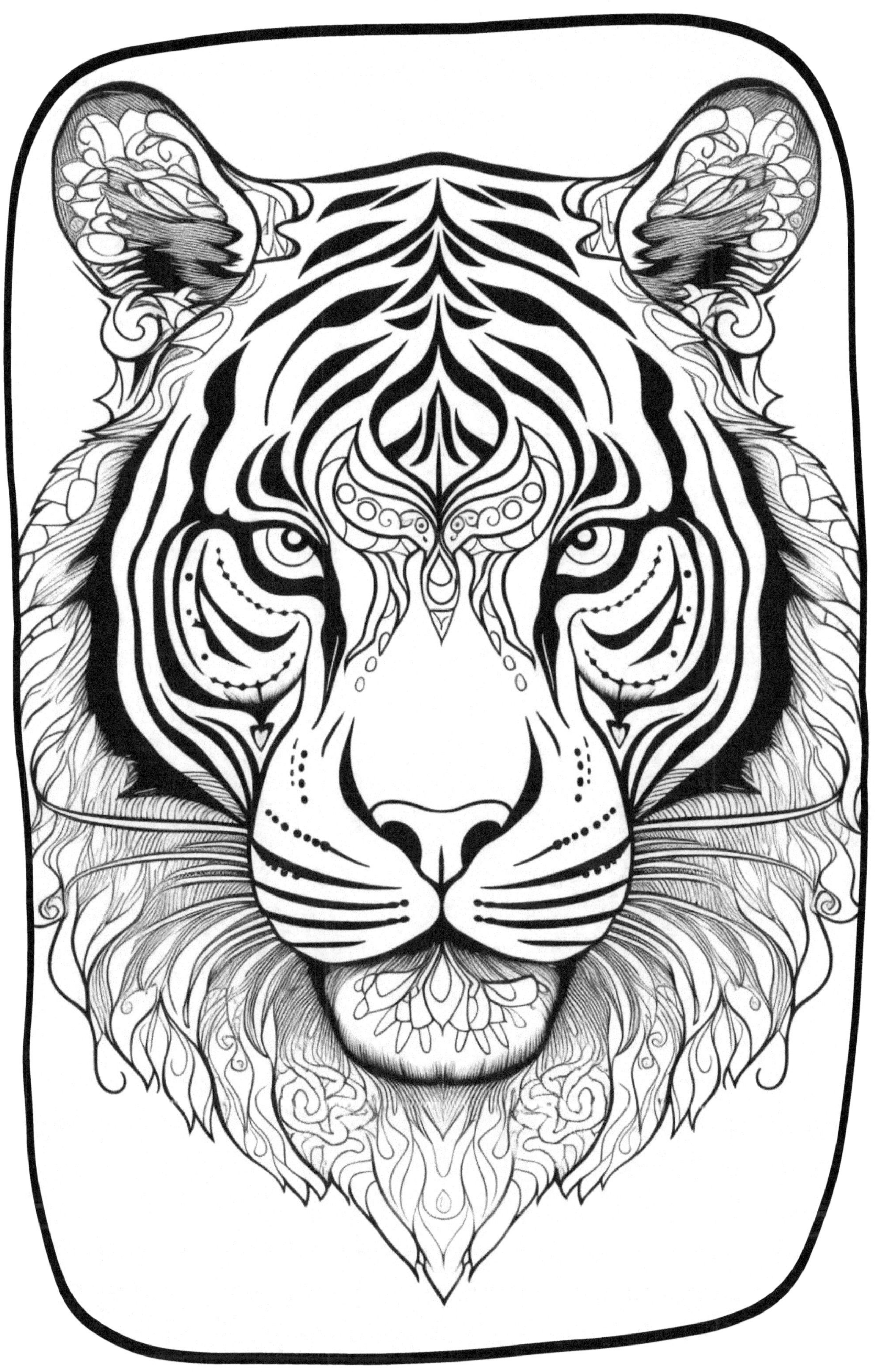

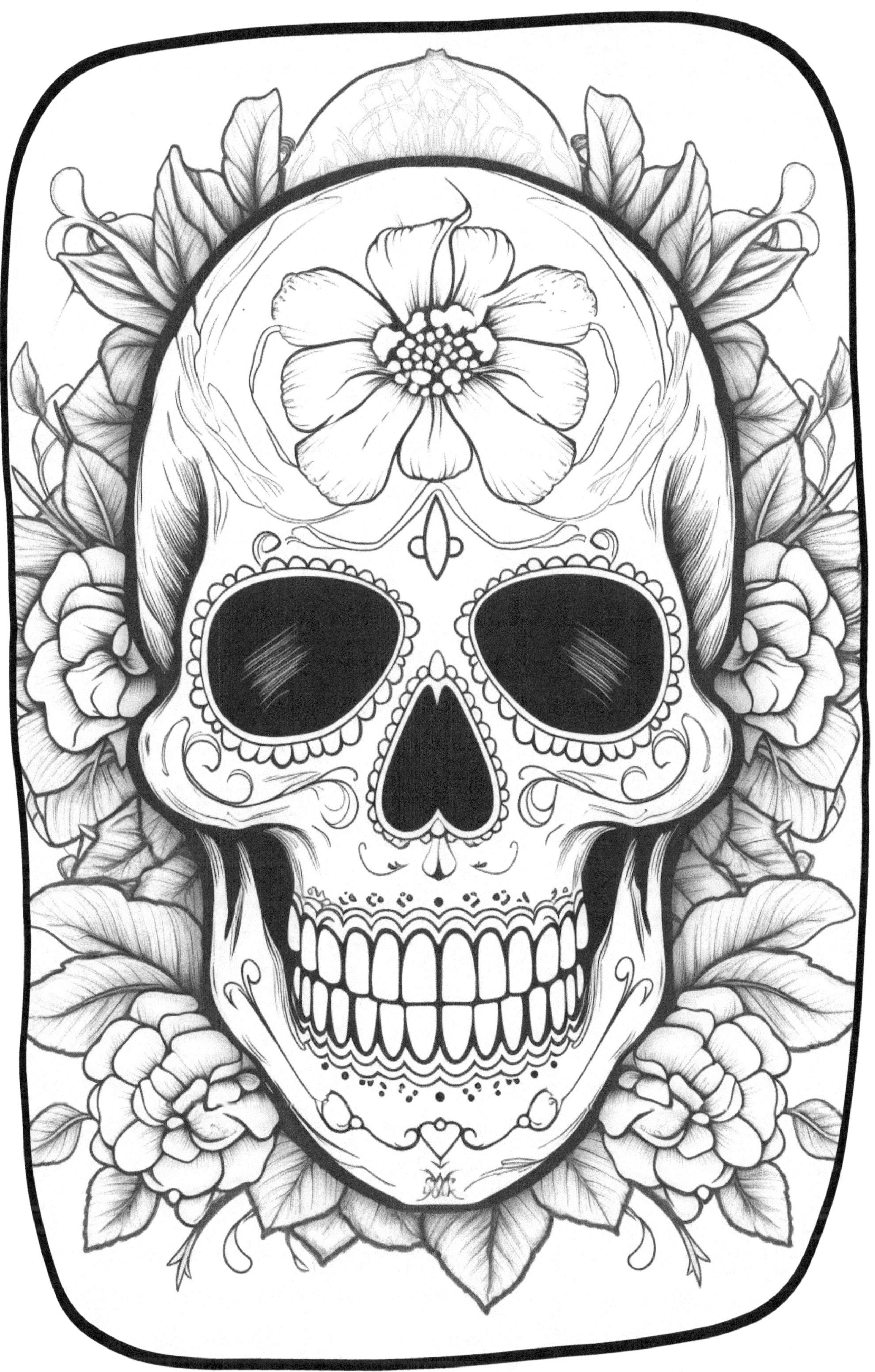

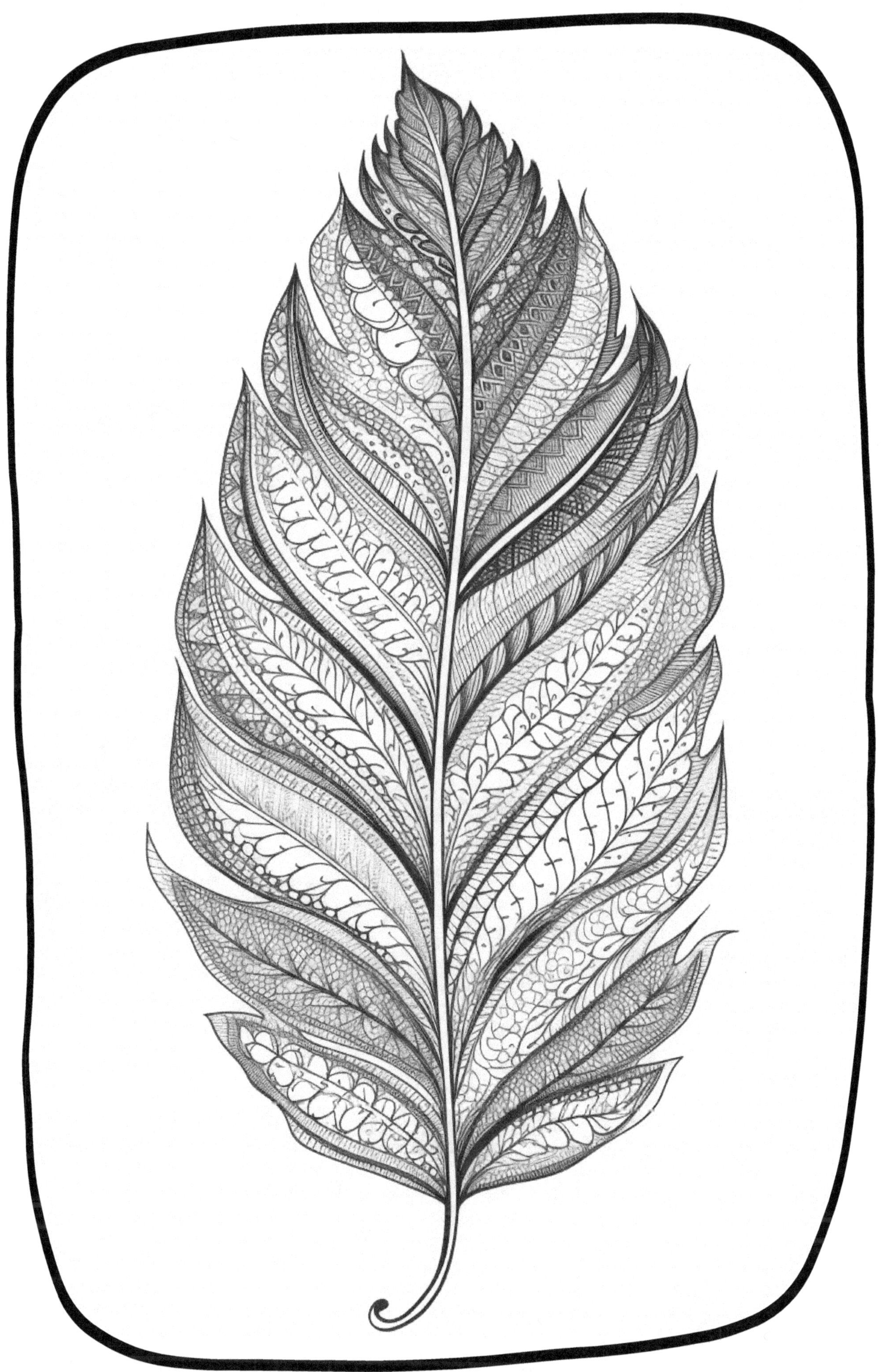

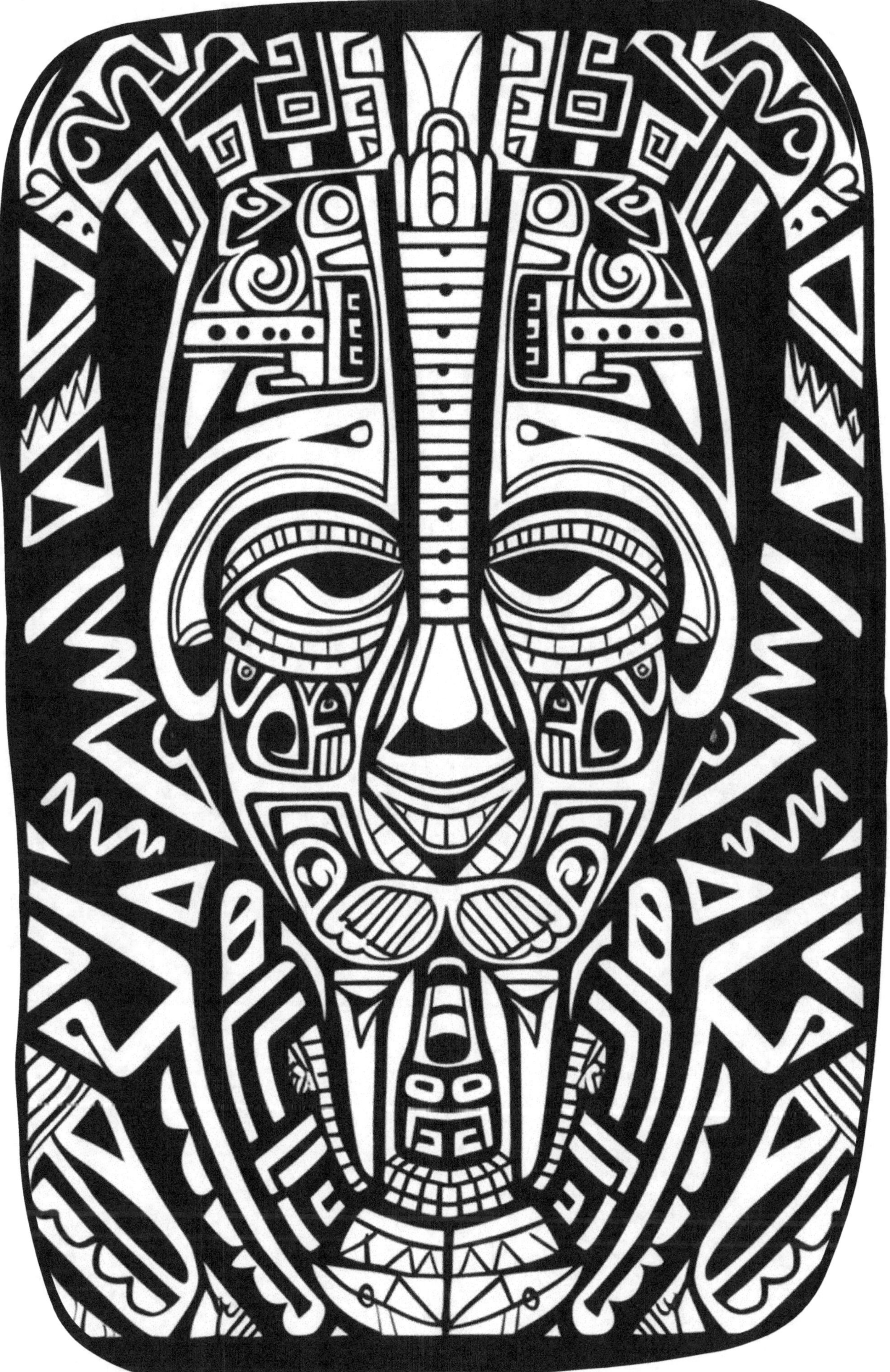

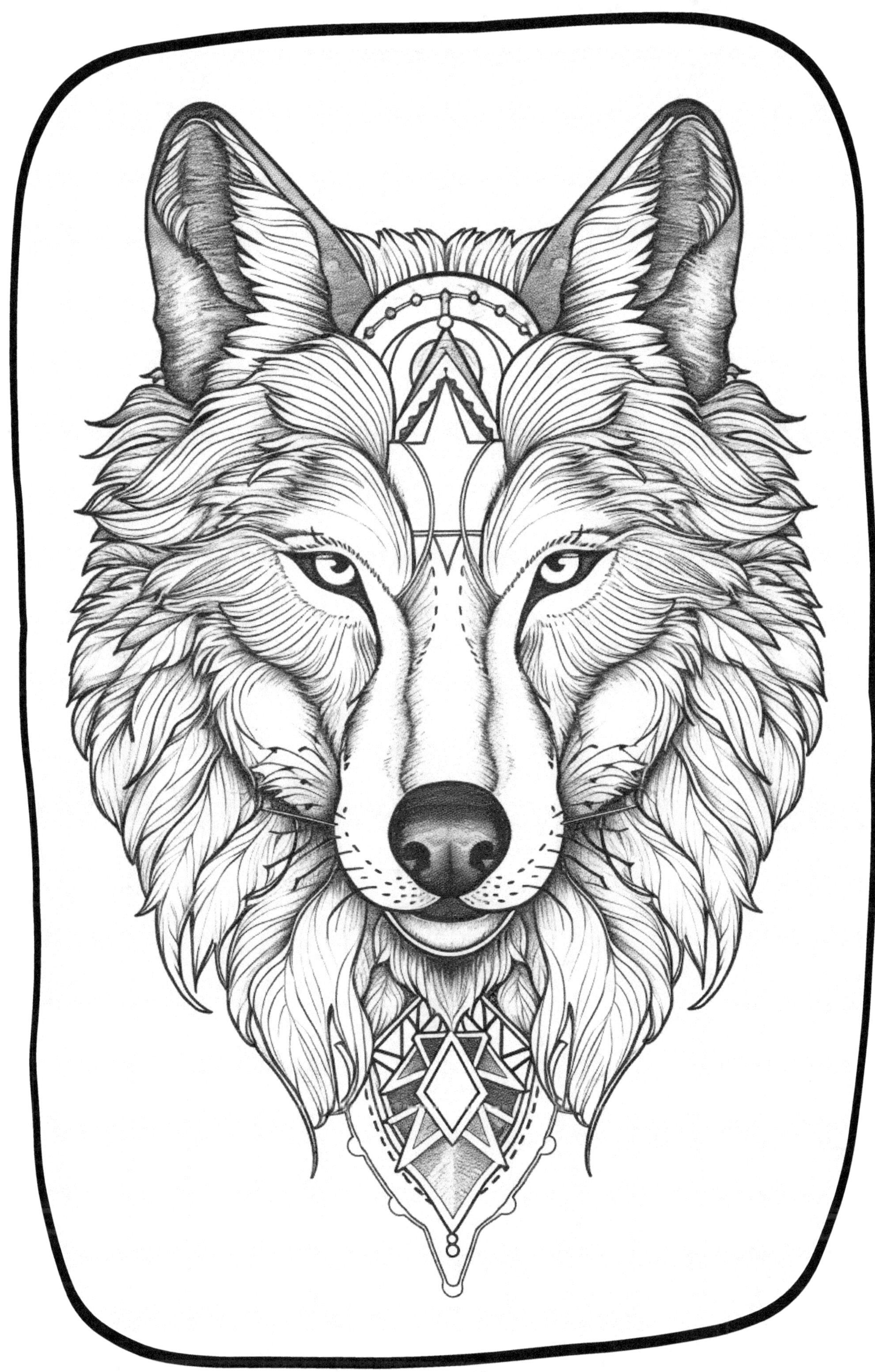

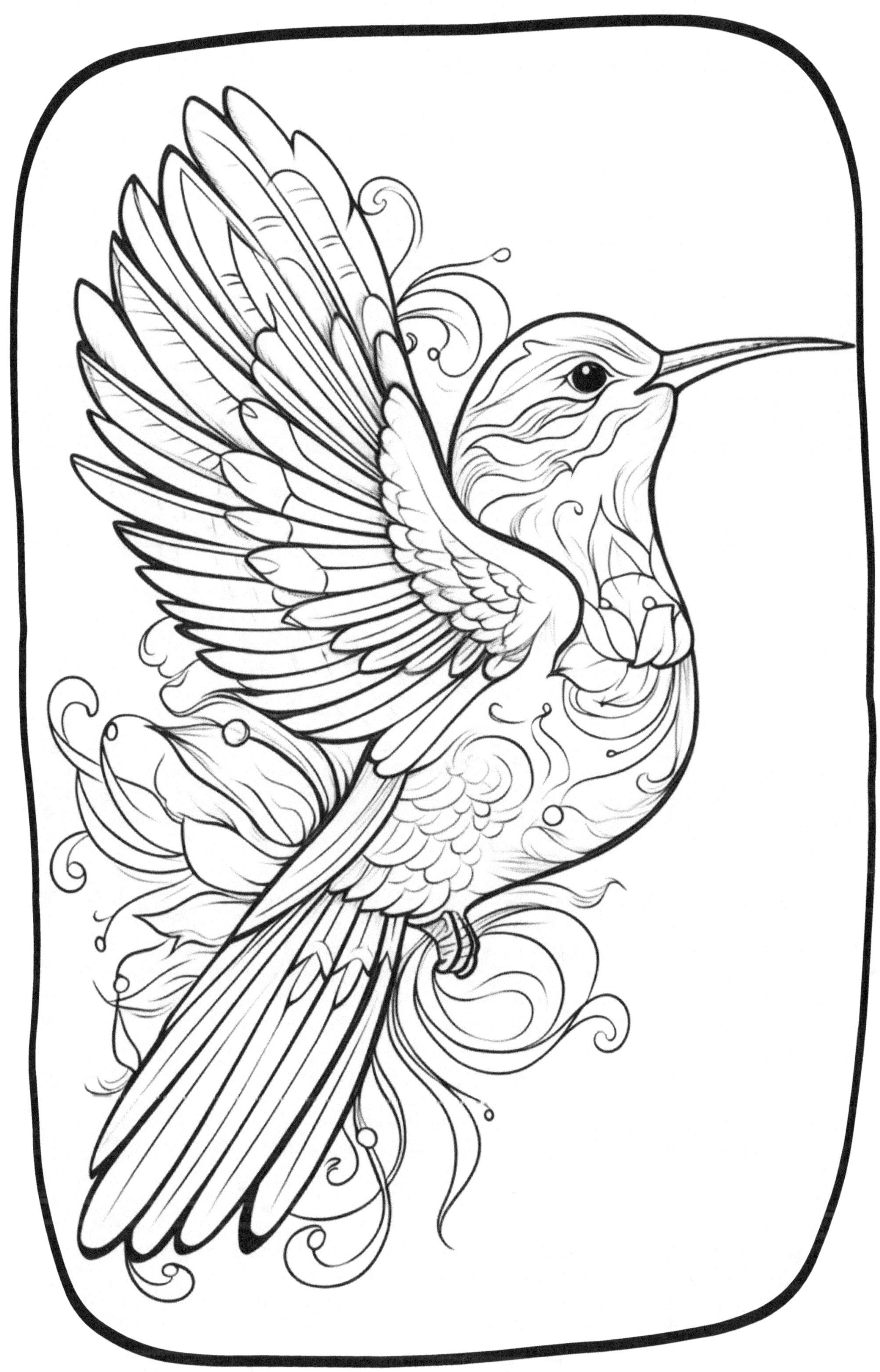

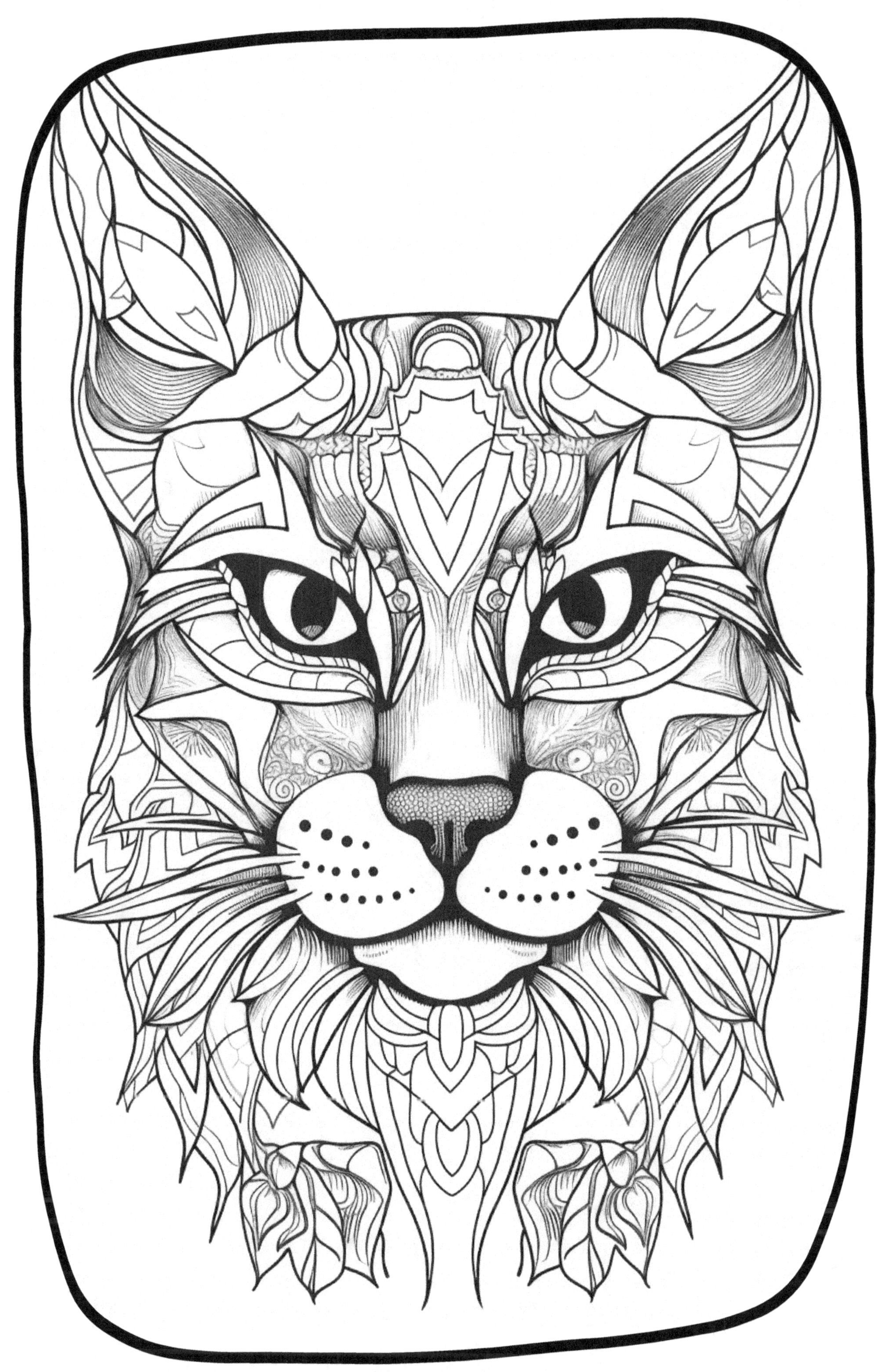

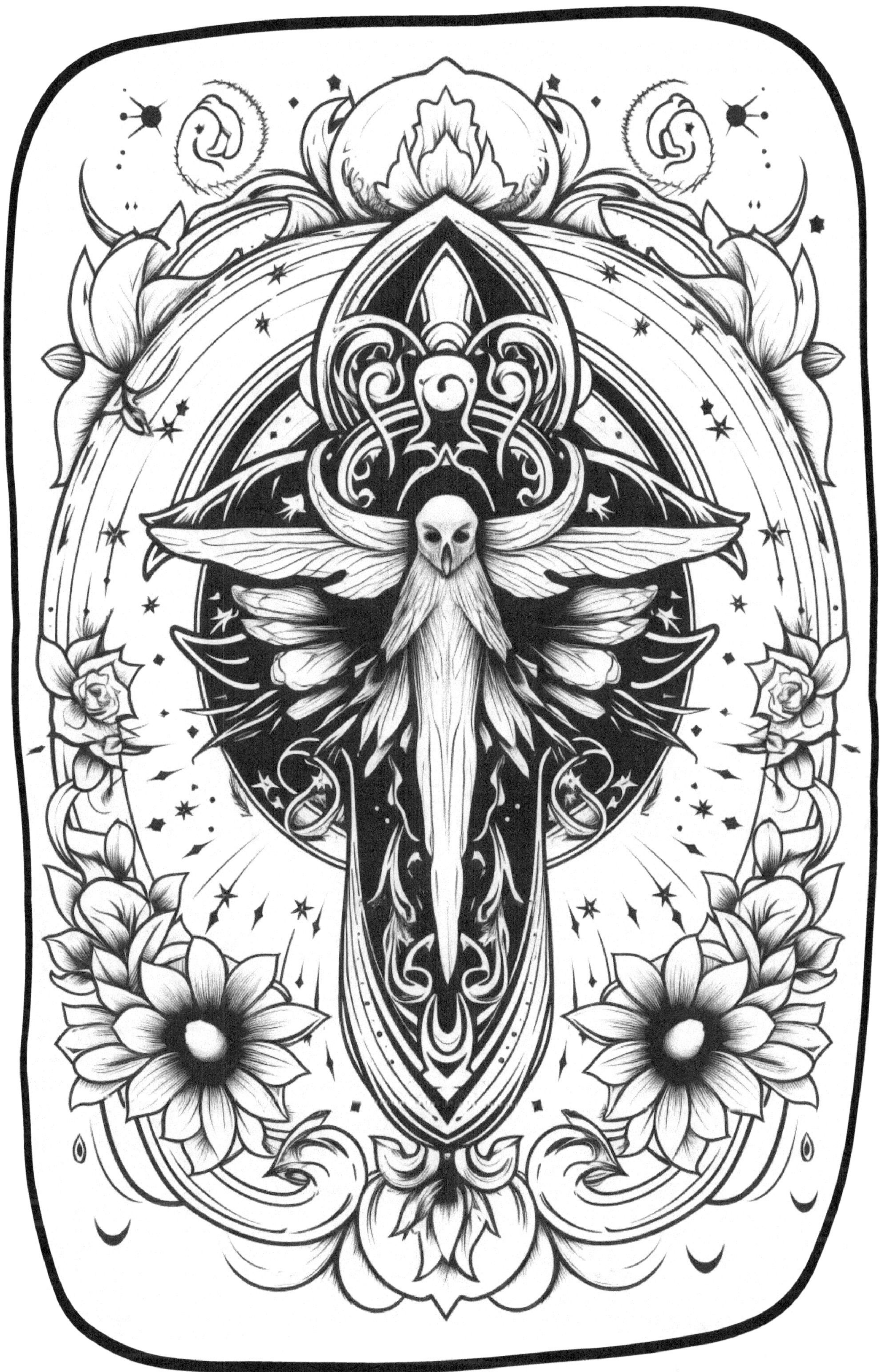

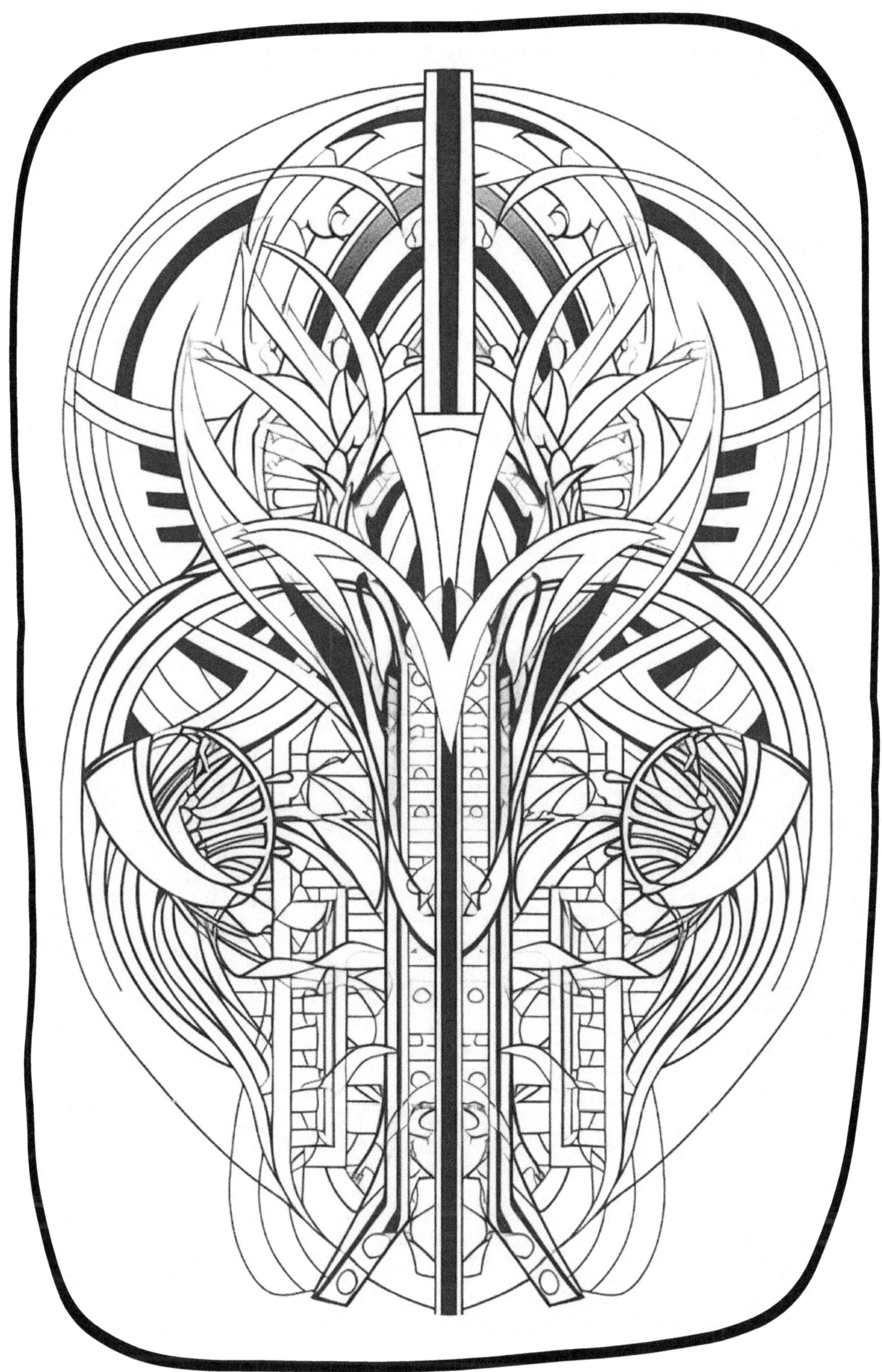